Disclaimer

The publisher of this book is by no way associated with the National Institute of Standards and Technology (NIST). The NIST did not publish this book. It was published by 50 page publications under the public domain license.

50 Page Publications.

Book Title: Camera Calibration for a Manufacturing Inspection Workstation

Book Author: Tsung-Ming Tsai;

Book Abstract: A CCD camera mounted on a manufacturing part inspection workstation is calibrated for measuring 3D part geometry. It is calibrated by using computer algorithms to analyze data collected from a specially designed calibration image pattern. The calibration image used is a black and white checkerboard pattern. A commonly used camera calibration procedure is used to analyze the image data of the checkerboard calibration image. A camera model is obtained which contains intrinsic parameters representing the characteristic properties of the camera. The calibration is proven to result in a sub-pixel accuracy. A machine-part test specimen is chosen to demonstrate the accuracy of application of the camera model to predict geometrical feature locations of usual manufacturing parts. As a first trial, the experimental test shows that an accuracy on the order of 1 mm is easily attainable in predicting the feature locations, with the part being placed at a distance about 45 cm from the camera. Depending on the applications, special optical lens assembly may be designed to attach on the CCD camera and higher measurement accuracy of the feature locations may be obtained.

Citation: NIST Interagency/Internal Report (NISTIR) - 7197

Keyword: camera calibration;CCD camera measurement;coordinate measurement

NISTIR 7197

Camera Calibration for a Manufacturing Inspection Workstation

Tsai, T.

U. S. DEPARTMENT OF COMMERCE
Technology Administration
National Institute of Standards
 and Technology
Intelligent Systems Division
Gaithersburg, MD 20899-8230

National Institute of Standards
and Technology
Technology Administration
U.S. Department of Commerce

NISTIR 7197

Camera Calibration for a Manufacturing Inspection Workstation

Tsai, T.

U. S. DEPARTMENT OF COMMERCE
Technology Administration
National Institute of Standards
  and Technology
Intelligent Systems Division
Gaithersburg, MD 20899-8230

January 2005

U.S. DEPARTMENT OF COMMERCE
Donald L. Evans, Secretary

TECHNOLOGY ADMINISTRATION
Phillip J. Bond, Under Secretary for Technology

NATIONAL INSTITUTE OF STANDARDS
AND TECHNOLOGY
Arden L. Bement, Jr., Director

Camera Calibration for a Manufacturing Inspection Workstation

Tsungming Tsai

Intelligent Systems Division
National Institute of Standards and Technology
Gaithersburg, MD 20899-8230

Abstract

A CCD camera mounted on a manufacturing part inspection workstation is calibrated for measuring 3D part geometry. It is calibrated by using computer algorithms to analyze data collected from a specially designed calibration image pattern. The calibration image used is a black and white checkerboard pattern. A commonly used camera calibration procedure is used to analyze the image data of the checkerboard calibration image. A camera model is obtained which contains intrinsic parameters representing the characteristic properties of the camera. The calibration is proven to result in a sub-pixel accuracy. A machine part test specimen is chosen to demonstrate the accuracy of application of the camera model to predict geometrical feature locations of usual manufacturing parts. As a first trial, the experimental test shows that an accuracy on the order of 1 mm is easily attainable in predicting the feature locations, with the part being placed at a distance about 45 cm from the camera. Depending on the applications, special optical lens assembly may be designed to attach on the CCD camera and higher measurement accuracy of the feature locations may be obtained.

1. Introduction

Machined parts manufactured by machine tools constantly need to be inspected for their dimensional accuracy. Many measurement techniques have been thoroughly investigated. Such measurement techniques include the use of rulers, gages, micrometers, optical sensors, acoustic sensors and laser interferometers. Because the geometry of machine parts is often complex, how to use dimensional measurements to reconstruct object geometry becomes a complicated metrology problem. Dimensional measurement methods that would sufficiently solve complicated metrology problems are frequently explored. Recently, the development of high performance CCD (Charge Coupled Device) image cameras allows advanced imaging measurement in many areas of application[1]. Use of these CCD cameras is still new for part inspection in the manufacturing industry. Many problems concerning the measurement

---

[1] Certain commercial equipment, instruments, or materials are identified in this paper to foster understanding. Such identification does not imply recommendation or endorsement by the National Institute of Standards and Technology, nor does it imply that the materials or equipment identified are necessarily the best available for the purpose.

accuracy and effectiveness of CCD camera imaging systems need to be clarified with experimental studies.

Coordinate measuring machines (CMM) have been widely used in industry for the 3D measurement of object geometry. Advanced CMM technology can now achieve high precision measurement [3]. In our laboratory, an inspection workstation has been installed as a test bed for dimensional measurement metrology experimentation. The inspection workstation is basically a coordinate measuring machine. A primary goal of the work on the workstation is to conduct an investigation on how CCD imaging cameras would add new capabilities to dimensional measurement of machined parts on the CMM. Capabilities such as object feature recognition, simultaneous multi-dimensional position and orientation measurements, and 2D and 3D object geometry mapping, are somewhat unique to CCD cameras.

To see how a CCD imaging camera will perform in the measurement of dimensions and features of a machined part, experiments need to be done. But before a camera can be put in use for measurement, it must be calibrated. In this experiment, we conduct a camera calibration on a CCD imaging camera mounted on a CMM for machined part inspection. Usually, the calibration starts with the collection of camera image data from a set of specially designed calibration image patterns. Computer programs are then written to process and analyze the calibration image data in conjunction with some additional ground truth information on the calibration image patterns. There are many camera calibration procedures that have been developed for industrial applications. Our work at this time is not to develop new camera calibration procedures, but to apply existing ones to calibrate the CCD camera on our part inspection workstation for use in later experiments.

As required by later experiments designed to evaluate how a CCD camera will perform on our current CMM installation, we now conduct a calibration on the camera using calibration procedures that already exist in the literature [1,2,4,5,7,8]. In particular, we use the camera calibration computer programs developed by J. Y. Bouguet [1] of California Institute of Technology. Camera calibration procedures vary in complexity, computation time, efficiency and accuracy. Depending on the need of an application, it is often necessary to trade off accuracy with computation time. Bouguet's procedure appears to be simple, efficient, and fast enough. It is able to provide the calibration results with sub-pixel accuracy. This kind of accuracy is good enough for our current experiment in the measurement of object features.

Conducting a camera calibration will serve many purposes. First, the correctness and effectiveness of a camera calibration procedure will be verified with experimental data. Since a camera calibration procedure may be used for many camera setups in various experiments, the calibration done with our camera setup may also serve as a demonstration of the calibration procedure for others. Most importantly, a camera calibration determines the measurement accuracy of the camera imaging system. Throughout the calibration process, possible sources of measurement errors may be identified. Doing a camera calibration will also verify the measurement repeatability and capability of the camera imaging system. Finally, a camera model can be obtained after the calibration. A camera model is a representation of the relation between the pixel coordinates of an object's image and the physical coordinates of the object.

Building a camera model is different from the determination of measurement accuracy; it models the camera's behavior in performing image transformation. A calibrated camera model is very useful later in the measurements of object locations and feature geometry through camera images.

As a note about the significant figures used in the data presentation of this report, the number of significant figures representing the accuracy in physical dimensions is only up to 0.5 mm, and that for pixel coordinates is only up to 0.3 pixel (see Eq. 13). However, for the purpose of preserving numerical computation accuracy, four or more decimal points are used to represent distance and pixel count in the calculation.

2. Calibration Image Data Collection

The purpose of camera calibration is to correlate the pixel coordinates on the camera image plane with the physical coordinates of a calibration target object. So the selection of a calibration target object should be one for which it is easy to determine the physical coordinates of the feature locations of particular interest. Also, on the camera image plane of this calibration object, the corresponding pixel coordinates of the selected feature locations of interest should be easily determined with a high degree of precision.

The simplest calibration target image pattern is a checkerboard image which consists of adjacent black and white squares. The easily identifiable features of this type of calibration image are the corners between the black and white squares. The pixel coordinates of the corners on the calibration image can be retrieved by corner finding computer algorithms. And the physical coordinates of the corners on the calibration target object can be determined by measuring the position of the corners with a scale or other more accurate methods. In this experiment, a scale was used. Because the calibration parameters of a camera may be non-uniform, i.e. not constant, over the wide volume or planar area of its viewing range, specific design of the calibration image pattern may be necessary. The symmetry of the evenly spaced squares of a checkerboard calibration pattern can provide a basis for detection of the non-uniformity of the camera characteristic properties. A calibration image with a single square would not be able to detect small variations of the camera properties over its wide viewing range. For a specific camera, there may be an ideal or optimum checkerboard size or density.

The checkerboard calibration image pattern used for this experiment was generated by a computer program and printed on regular printer paper. It consists of 10 squares in the x direction and 8 squares in the y direction. The total length in the x direction is 260.9 mm and that in the y direction is 198.5 mm. A simple calculation gives the dimensions of each square to be 26.09 mm in the x direction and 24.82 mm in the y direction. This checkerboard image was then pasted on a rigid aluminum plate so that its position and orientation could be changed through various translational and rotational rigid body motions. Because the computer program which generated the checkerboard pattern programmed each square with exactly the same dimension, assuming the printer hardware was uniform on the printing surface and does not distort the printed image, the final printed image should be correctly spaced and uniform. Of course there always is some distortion in the final calibration image pattern, some corners may be off, but we will assume errors of the corner positions are within the tolerance of our experiment.

To begin the image data collection process, this checkerboard calibration image was placed under the CCD camera. The CCD camera head unit scans the optical intensity of the object image captured from the aperture and lenses. Inside the camera, the CCD sensor area contains a 640 x 480 array of image pixels which convert optical intensity into electrical signals. These electrical signals were then passed through a camera control unit so that the image signal was converted to digital color information data -- red, green, and blue. Inside the camera control unit, the color information was finally converted into the YUV format for easier data transmission into computer systems. A computer equipped with a video card was used to collect the image data coming from the camera control unit. An image library software package named XIL was then used as the interface between the video card and the rest of the image processing programs. The XIL image library routines interpret the YUV image data format collected inside the video card and convert the YUV image data into XIL's own internal image format. The image library routine has the options of choosing either color image format or black and white image format. Since our checkerboard was black and white, the black and white image format was used. Inside XIL, each image collected was stored into a 640 x 480 array of memory. Each array element records the value of a corresponding image pixel. The image data inside each 640 x 480 memory array can then be displayed on the computer screen or saved to a disk file.

Since the objects to be inspected may be located in a wide region in front of the camera, the calibration image pattern should be placed to cover all the areas of interest. In this experiment, ten calibration images were collected as shown in Figs. A1 – A10 of Appendix A. These ten images were obtained by placing the checkerboard calibration image surface at various positions and orientations by moving the aluminum plate through different translational and rotational rigid body motions respectively. Each of these images was digitalized and stored in computer memory as a 640 x 480 pixel array. The pixel data information corresponding to each calibration image was then saved to a disk file for later usage and processing.

3. Corner Finding on the Calibration Images

Camera calibration involves correlation of the pixel coordinates of points in the camera image of an object and the physical coordinates of the corresponding points on the object. Thus, point locations become the focus of our study. Usually, not every point is required to do the calibration, but a set of sampled points on the object and a set of the corresponding points in the image are needed. In the calibration data sampling process, questions about which are the appropriate points to select and how to select them need to be determined first. To establish the correspondence between the pixel coordinates of the image of an object and the physical coordinates of the object, point locations must be identified in the image and on the object, and the mapping between the corresponding point locations also be identified. In short, the key to the problem is to identify which point in the image corresponds to which point on the object. A point usually has certain properties associated with it, such as coordinates, material property, color, etc. Points are distinguished by the different values of their associated properties. A set of adjacent points with a variety of property values forms a recognizable feature. Furthermore, the location of a point inside a particular feature can be determined by the different property values of its neighboring points. Since features are recognizable, identifying the same features that appear both in the image and on the object becomes a good way to establish the mapping relation of point locations.

The design of the checkerboard calibration image provides a simple way to precisely locate the relevant feature point location for camera image calibration. Corners of the black and white squares on the checkerboard calibration image become the best way of precisely identifying the feature point location. Computer algorithms available in the literature were implemented into our system to find these corners from the image pixel data of the checkerboard calibration images placed at various positions and orientations. The black and white squares on the calibration images clearly mark the locations of their corners, and thus allow the computer algorithms to easily locate the corners.

J. Y. Bouguet of the Vision Group in California Institute of Technology has written a computer program in MATLAB which finds corners of the checkerboard images [1]. His program is used here for our experiment of the CCD camera calibration procedure for manufactured part inspection. The program interpolates the pixel image data with sub-pixel values, finds the gradient of the image and then finds the pixel locations of the corners. Sub-pixel accuracy of the corner locations may be obtained.

The corner finding program locates a corner by recognizing the four black and white squares surrounding the corner. The program sets a window around each corner and tries to find the pixel coordinates. Within the window, the four edges of the black and white squares must be clearly recognizable by the corner finding program. Otherwise, the corner finding program will be confused and the results it finds inaccurate. On the boundary of the checkerboard image pattern, a special design on the border squares may be required so that they have some extra extensions and each corner on the border is surrounded by the four edges of the black and white squares within the window of the corner finding program. There are 10 x 8 = 80 squares detected by the corner extraction routines, which have 11 x 9 = 99 corners to find. The corner finding procedure was performed on each of the ten calibration images, and the results are listed in Tables B1 – B10 for each calibration image. The pixel coordinates of the corners found by the computer program are re-projected back and marked with cross signs on the respective checkerboard calibration images, as shown in Figures A1 – A10. The re-projected corners on a checkerboard image can be further examined for re-projection accuracy by zooming in the image around each individual corner with various amplification factors as shown in Figs. 1 – 4. The thick and thin corner markers in the zoomed images give more insight to the sub-pixel resolution of extracted corners. For comparison, the physical coordinates of the corners of the checkerboard calibration image are also listed in Table B0, which are calculated from the measured dimension of each square.

Fig. 1   Original Image to be Zoomed at Grid No. (6, 5) , Zoom-in Factor = 1.0

Fig. 2   Zoomed Image at Grid No. (6, 5) ,   Zoom-in Factor = 2.5

Fig. 3   Zoomed Image at Grid No. (6, 5) , Zoom-in Factor = 5.0

Fig. 4   Zoomed Image at Grid No. (6, 5) , Zoom-in Factor = 10.0

4. Calibration Matrix (Camera Model) Calculations

Variations of pixel coordinates of the image of an object depend on several factors, such as (1) focal length of the camera lens, (2) position and orientation of the imaging plane of the CCD sensor with respect to the optical axis of the camera, (3) distortion due to the camera lenses, and (4) location of the object being imaged. These factors can be separated into two sets: intrinsic and extrinsic. The intrinsic factors are due to the camera characteristics, e.g. focal length, imaging plane position and orientation, lens distortion, etc., which are independent of the object location. Extrinsic factors are due to the translational and rotational rigid body motion of the object, which are independent of the camera characteristics.

A camera model can be constructed by using the information from the camera image of an object and its physical location. The pixel coordinates of feature point locations in the image and the physical coordinates of the corresponding feature point locations on the object together contain all the information about the correlation between the two. The correlation includes changes due to the effect of the intrinsic factors and that of the extrinsic factors. The effect due to the intrinsic factors may be de-coupled from the effect due to the extrinsic factors in a simple fashion. This correlation can be expressed in a mathematical formulation in which the effect of the intrinsic factors is modeled with a set of parameters, called intrinsic parameters; and the effect of the extrinsic factors is modeled with another set of parameters, called extrinsic parameters. Knowing the intrinsic parameters, a set of pixel coordinates on the image can be calculated from the physical coordinates of the respective point locations on the object. The calculated pixel coordinates on the image are then compared to the measured pixel coordinates on the image. The error between the calculated and the measured pixel coordinates represents the accuracy of the camera model.

Point locations in the image are identified by features containing them. Locations of the feature points in the image change when the locations of the corresponding feature points on the object change. Therefore, point locations of the features on the object become the determining variables in the correlation formulation between the image and the object. Since the object of interest is rigid, relative distances among the point locations of the features on the object will not change with respect to the object itself. Any changes of the point locations of the features on the object would be due to the rigid body motion of the object, which would be only the translation and rotation of the object. For the purpose of performing the camera calibration, the same set of features on one object can be used, with the object being moved to various locations, or different features on many different objects can be used. In this experiment, we use the former approach. In the calibration procedure, feature point locations both in the image and on the object are known, and camera model parameters, i.e. the intrinsic parameters and the extrinsic parameters, are the final unknowns to be determined. If the intrinsic parameters are already determined by any means, then the only parameters left to be determined in the correlation formulation between the pixel coordinates on the image and the physical coordinates on the object are the extrinsic parameters. These extrinsic parameters are just the parameters describing the translational and rotational rigid body motion of the object. In other words, if the intrinsic parameters of the camera model are known, then changes in the point locations of the features on the image can be used to determine the amount of rigid body translational and rotational motion that the object has undergone.

If both the intrinsic and extrinsic parameters are unknown, then an iterative procedure must be taken to determine them using the information of the pixel coordinates of feature point locations on the image and the physical coordinates of the corresponding point locations on the object. First, an initial approximation of the intrinsic parameters is assumed, and the corresponding extrinsic parameters are determined. A set of pixel coordinates of the feature point locations on the image is then calculated from the physical coordinates of the corresponding feature point locations on the object using the first set of intrinsic and extrinsic parameters resulting from the first step of the iteration. The errors between the calculated pixel coordinates and the measured pixel coordinates of the feature point locations are then used to determine the next set of approximated values of the intrinsic parameters. The next iteration produces the next set of the extrinsic parameters. The iteration process continues until the errors between the calculated pixel coordinates and the measured pixel coordinates of the feature coordinates are minimized. The final sets of the intrinsic and extrinsic parameters obtained when the pixel errors are minimized are the desired results of this camera calibration procedure. When we say the errors are minimized, it means that the errors reach stable values after successive iteration steps and the differences between the errors of successive steps fall below specified tolerances. The formulation used in the computer program that calculates the intrinsic and extrinsic parameters is described below. The mathematical equations used in the formulation represent the numerical algorithms actually used in the computer programs. The numerical algorithms used here are those of Bouguet. But the equations and descriptions of the following formulation are written according to our experimental setup. They are different from those of Bouguet, although the equations may be equivalent. The physical quantities of this experiment which are associated with the parameters used in the following formulation are also identified.

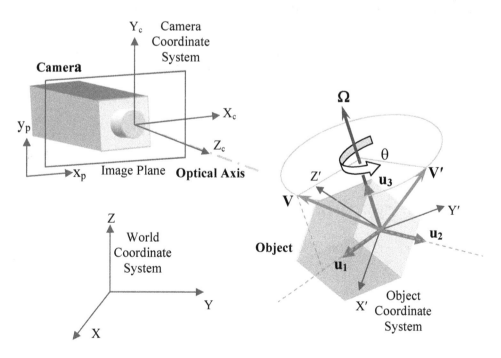

Fig. 5   Object Orientation and Rodrigues Rotation Vector

9

The camera projects the geometry of an object in 3D space onto an image plane located behind the lenses of the camera. This camera imaging transformation can be expressed in terms of a mathematical transformation model. First, we define a reference coordinate frame, (X_c, Y_c, Z_c), which is fixed on the camera system, with Z_c-axis pointing outward from the lenses and along the camera optical axis (Fig. 5). Any point, P, on the object will have coordinates, $P = (X_c, Y_c, Z_c)$, with respect to the camera reference frame. Secondly, a point on the image plane is assigned a set of 2D pixel coordinates, (x_p, y_p). The camera imaging transformation projects the 3D coordinates, (X_c, Y_c, Z_c), in the camera reference frame, into the 2D pixel coordinates, (x_p, y_p), on the image plane. The mathematical model assumes that the projection transformation begins with a normalization on the 3D coordinates, (X_c, Y_c, Z_c), dividing the X_c and Y_c components by the Z_c component, yielding a set of 2D normalized coordinates, $x_n = (x, y)$, as defined in Eq. 1. We call (x, y) the tangential coordinates, and Eq.1a defines the radial coordinate, r.

$$x_n = \begin{pmatrix} X_c / Z_c \\ \\ Y_c / Z_c \end{pmatrix} = \begin{pmatrix} x \\ \\ y \end{pmatrix} \qquad \text{(Eq. 1)}$$

$$r^2 = x^2 + y^2 \qquad \text{(Eq. 1a)}$$

Due to imperfection of the lenses, the camera imaging projection will contain a noticeable amount of distortion in the image transformation. Instead of the undistorted normalized coordinates, x_n, a set of distorted normalized coordinates, $x_d = (x_d(1), x_d(2))$, needs to be used to model the camera distortion effects. The relation between x_n and x_d, as described in Eq. 2, models the distortion effects in the camera imaging transformation. The first term in Eq. 2 models the radial distortion and the second term, dx, models the tangential distortion. Eq. 3 defines the tangential distortion, dx, in relation to the undistorted normalized coordinates, x_n. As can be seen from Eqs. 2 and 3, the radial distortion is modeled by multiplying the undistorted normalized coordinates, x_n, by a radial distortion factor which consists of a polynomial in r^2, with the coefficients $k_c(1), k_c(2), k_c(5)$ being the distortion factors. In Eq. 3, dx models the tangential distortion which consists of second order polynomials in radial coordinate, r, and tangential coordinates, x, y, with the coefficients being the distortion factors, $k_c(3)$ and $k_c(4)$.

$$x_d = \begin{pmatrix} x_d(1) \\ \\ x_d(2) \end{pmatrix} = (1 + k_c(1)*r^2 + k_c(2)*r^4 + k_c(5)*r^6) * x_n + dx \qquad \text{(Eq. 2)}$$

$$dx = \begin{pmatrix} 2*k_c(3)*x*y + k_c(4)*(r^2 + 2*x^2) \\ \\ k_c(3)*(r^2 + 2*y^2) + 2*k_c(4)*x*y \end{pmatrix} \qquad \text{(Eq. 3)}$$

$$\begin{pmatrix} x_p \\ \\ y_p \end{pmatrix} = \begin{pmatrix} f_c(1)*(x_d(1) + \alpha_c*x_d(2)) + c_c(1) \\ \\ f_c(2)*x_d(2) + c_c(2) \end{pmatrix} \qquad \text{(Eq. 4)}$$

With the distortion model being incorporated into x_d, the final pixel coordinates, (x_p, y_p), of a point on the image plane are just a simple linear transformation from the distorted normalized coordinates, x_d, as described in Eq. 4. In matrix form, this linear transformation is described in Eq. 5. The coefficients, $f_c(1)$ and $f_c(2)$, model the focal lengths of the camera in the x and y directions. The skew coefficient α_c defines the angle between the x, y pixel axes on the image plane. The coefficients $c_c(1)$ and $c_c(2)$ model the location of a principal point which may roughly represent the center of the image [6].

Both the distortion factors in the distortion model, Eqs. 3 and 4, and the projection parameters in the image projection model, Eq. 5, depend only on the camera internal characteristic properties and are thus called intrinsic parameters.

$$\begin{pmatrix} x_p \\ y_p \\ 1 \end{pmatrix} = \begin{pmatrix} K \end{pmatrix} * \begin{pmatrix} x_d(1) \\ x_d(2) \\ 1 \end{pmatrix} \qquad \text{(Eq. 5)}$$

$$\begin{pmatrix} K \end{pmatrix} = \begin{pmatrix} f_c(1) & \alpha_c*f_c(1) & c_c(1) \\ 0 & f_c(2) & c_c(2) \\ 0 & 0 & 1 \end{pmatrix} \qquad \text{(Eq. 6)}$$

The position and orientation of objects are normally expressed in a world coordinate frame. A relation thus needs to be established between the world coordinates of an object and its camera coordinates. For convenience, an object coordinate frame is also set up for the object geometry description. Let $XX = (X, Y, Z)$ be the coordinates of a point, P, in the world coordinate frame, and $XX_o = (X', Y', Z')$ its coordinates in the object coordinate frame. The object coordinates, XX_o, are related to the coordinates, $XX_c = (X_c, Y_c, Z_c)$, of the point P in the camera reference frame by a coordinate transformation, Eq. 7. If the camera is stationary, then XX and XX_c differ only by a constant transformation. The coordinate transformation between XX_o and XX_c represents the relative positions and orientations of the object with respect to the camera reference frame, which are the results of the translational and rotational rigid body motion of the object with respect to the camera reference frame. The translational motion of the object is modeled by the translation vector, T_c, in Eq. 7, and the rotational motion by the rotation matrix, R_c.

$$XX_c = R_c * XX_o + T_c \qquad \text{(Eq. 7)}$$

As an object moves relative to the camera, its image on the image plane changes. This change in image is only due to the motion of the object and is independent of the camera intrinsic characteristics. As described previously, factors that result in this kind of change are extrinsic factors. Eq. 7 models the correlation between changes in the image and the object motion. The rotation matrix, R_c, and the translation vector, T_c, in the object motion model,

Eq 7, are explicit expressions of the extrinsic parameters. Corresponding to each of the calibration images, Figs. A1 – A10, there is one individual rotation matrix, Rc_k, and one individual translation vector, Tc_k, where k = 1, 2, 3, ... , 10. A rotation vector, Om = ($\tilde{\omega}_x$, $\tilde{\omega}_y$, $\tilde{\omega}_z$), is also used to describe certain types of rotational motion of the object, which are sufficient in this experiment. The rotational vector, Om, can be converted to the rotational matrix, R_c, and vice versa, through the Rodrigues formula [1], Eq. 8.

$$
R_c = \begin{pmatrix} \cos\tilde{\theta} & 0 & 0 \\ 0 & \cos\tilde{\theta} & 0 \\ 0 & 0 & \cos\tilde{\theta} \end{pmatrix} + \begin{pmatrix} 0 & -\tilde{\omega}_z & \tilde{\omega}_y \\ \tilde{\omega}_z & 0 & -\tilde{\omega}_x \\ -\tilde{\omega}_y & \tilde{\omega}_x & 0 \end{pmatrix} (\sin\tilde{\theta}/\tilde{\theta})
$$

$$
+ \begin{pmatrix} \tilde{\omega}_x^2 & \tilde{\omega}_x\tilde{\omega}_y & \tilde{\omega}_x\tilde{\omega}_z \\ \tilde{\omega}_y\tilde{\omega}_x & \tilde{\omega}_y^2 & \tilde{\omega}_y\tilde{\omega}_z \\ \tilde{\omega}_z\tilde{\omega}_x & \tilde{\omega}_z\tilde{\omega}_y & \tilde{\omega}_z^2 \end{pmatrix} (1-\cos\tilde{\theta})/\tilde{\theta}^2 \qquad \text{(Eq. 8)}
$$

where $\tilde{\theta} = \sqrt{\tilde{\omega}_x^2 + \tilde{\omega}_y^2 + \tilde{\omega}_z^2}$

The relationships among the rotation vector, Rodrigues rotation matrix, and object orientation are more easily seen from Fig. 5 by setting up a coordinate system (u_1, u_2, u_3), in which the u_3-axis is aligned with the rotation vector, Ω. For any vector, V, which is to be transformed to V' by a rotation of angle θ about the Ω-axis, the u_2-axis is defined to be the unit vector of $\Omega \times V$. The other axis, u_1, of the rotation coordinate system is defined to be the unit vector of $\Omega \times (\Omega \times V)$. Thus, $u_1 = \Omega \times (\Omega \times V) / |\Omega \times (\Omega \times V)|$, $u_2 = \Omega \times V / |\Omega \times V|$, and $u_3 = \Omega / |\Omega|$. In the coordinate system (X, Y, Z), we denote the components of Ω as (ω_x, ω_y, ω_z), those of V as (V_x, V_y, V_z), and those of the unit vector, V / |V|, as (v_x, v_y, v_z). We also denote φ as the angle between V and Ω. Then it can be shown that the unit vectors (u_1, u_2, u_3), when expressed in the world coordinate system, are given by the following equations.

$$
u_1 = \frac{-1}{\omega^2 \sin\varphi} \begin{pmatrix} 0 & -\omega_z & \omega_y \\ \omega_z & 0 & -\omega_x \\ -\omega_y & \omega_x & 0 \end{pmatrix} \begin{pmatrix} 0 & -\omega_z & \omega_y \\ \omega_z & 0 & -\omega_x \\ -\omega_y & \omega_x & 0 \end{pmatrix} \begin{pmatrix} v_x \\ v_y \\ v_z \end{pmatrix} \qquad \text{(Eq. 9a)}
$$

$$
u_2 = \frac{1}{\omega \sin\varphi} \begin{pmatrix} 0 & -\omega_z & \omega_y \\ \omega_z & 0 & -\omega_x \\ -\omega_y & \omega_x & 0 \end{pmatrix} \begin{pmatrix} v_x \\ v_y \\ v_z \end{pmatrix} \qquad \text{(Eq. 9b)}
$$

$$\mathbf{u_3} = \frac{1}{\omega^2 \cos\varphi} \begin{pmatrix} \omega_x^2 & \omega_x\omega_y & \omega_x\omega_z \\ \omega_y\omega_x & \omega_y^2 & \omega_y\omega_z \\ \omega_z\omega_x & \omega_z\omega_y & \omega_z^2 \end{pmatrix} \begin{pmatrix} V_x \\ V_y \\ V_z \end{pmatrix} \qquad \text{(Eq. 9c)}$$

Now we consider **V** and **V'** in both the world coordinate system (X, Y, Z) and the rotation coordinate system ($\mathbf{u_1}$, $\mathbf{u_2}$, $\mathbf{u_3}$). In the world coordinate system, **V** and **V'** are written as in Eqs. 10a, where ($\mathbf{e_x}$, $\mathbf{e_y}$, $\mathbf{e_z}$) are the unit vectors of X-, Y-, Z-axis respectively. In the rotation coordinate system, **V** and **V'** are written as in Eqs. 10b. The rotation of an angle θ around the $\mathbf{\Omega}$-vector relates (V_1, V_2, V_3) and (V'_1, V'_2, V'_3) by the matrix transformation of Eq. 11a. The same rotation relates (V_x, V_y, V_z) and (V'_x, V'_y, V'_z) by another matrix transformation, Eq. 11b, in which the rotation matrix, $\check{\mathbf{R}}$, is to be identified.

$$\left. \begin{aligned} \mathbf{V} &= V_x\mathbf{e_x} + V_y\mathbf{e_y} + V_z\mathbf{e_z} \\ \mathbf{V'} &= V'_x\mathbf{e_x} + V'_y\mathbf{e_y} + V'_z\mathbf{e_z} \end{aligned} \right\} \text{(Eqs. 10a)} \qquad \left. \begin{aligned} \mathbf{V} &= V_1\mathbf{e_1} + V_2\mathbf{e_2} + V_3\mathbf{e_3} \\ \mathbf{V'} &= V'_1\mathbf{e_1} + V'_2\mathbf{e_2} + V'_3\mathbf{e_3} \end{aligned} \right\} \text{(Eqs. 10b)}$$

$$\begin{pmatrix} V'_1 \\ V'_2 \\ V'_3 \end{pmatrix} = \begin{pmatrix} \cos\theta & -\sin\theta & 0 \\ \sin\theta & \cos\theta & 0 \\ 0 & 0 & 1 \end{pmatrix} \begin{pmatrix} V_1 \\ V_2 \\ V_3 \end{pmatrix} \text{(Eq.11a)} \qquad \begin{pmatrix} V'_x \\ V'_y \\ V'_z \end{pmatrix} = \begin{pmatrix} \check{\mathbf{R}} \end{pmatrix} \begin{pmatrix} V_x \\ V_y \\ V_z \end{pmatrix} \text{(Eq. 11b)}$$

If the camera coordinate system is placed at the same orientation as the world coordinate system, then ($\tilde{\omega}_x$, $\tilde{\omega}_y$, $\tilde{\omega}_z$) = (ω_x, ω_y, ω_z) and $\tilde{\theta} = \theta$. By substituting Eqs. 9 into Eqs. 10b, and by cross reference of Eqs. 10 to 11, it can be proved that the rotation matrix $\check{\mathbf{R}}$ is equal to the Rodrigues rotation matrix Rc. To better visualize the object orientation transformation, use the object coordinate system (X', Y', Z') which is fixed on the object as shown in Fig. 5. Originally, before any rotation, the direction of the object coordinate system (X', Y', Z') coincides with direction of the world coordinate system (X, Y, Z). After the object is rotated around the $\mathbf{\Omega}$-vector by an angle θ, the three object coordinate axes deviate away from the three world coordinate axes. The new orientation of each object coordinate axis is obtained by multiplying its corresponding world coordinate axis with the Rodrigues rotation matrix Rc.

Once we have modeled the correlation between the pixel image on the image plane and the geometry of an object of interest, the entire camera calibration problem reduces to the determination of the intrinsic parameters and the extrinsic parameters of the camera model. The following describes the procedures to determine the intrinsic and extrinsic parameters. The numerical procedures are the algorithms used by Bouguet. But the description is written according to the environment of our experimental setup, which is different from that of Bouguet. The format of this description strictly follows the major logical steps of the numerical algorithms presented above.

(1) Given an initial guess of the set of the intrinsic parameters, (c_c, f_c, α_c, k_c), compute the initial set of the extrinsic parameters, Om_k and Tc_k, for each image k, from the measured pixel coordinates of the feature corners on the image plane and the

13

known physical coordinates of the corresponding corner locations on the checkerboard calibration image.

(2) Then, the calculated initial set of extrinsic parameters, Om_k and Tc_k, is further refined through an iterative calculation procedure for each image, k, to result in a set of optimum extrinsic parameters based on the initial guess of the intrinsic parameters. The iterative process begins as follows. Knowing the initial values of the intrinsic parameters and the initial values of the extrinsic parameters, a set of projected pixel coordinates of the feature corners on the image plane, Xk_calculated, is calculated from the physical coordinates, X_checkerboard, of the corresponding corner locations on the checkerboard calibration image. The calculated pixel coordinates, Xk_calculated, are then compared with the measured pixel coordinates, Xk_measured. The measured pixel coordinates were obtained by extracting the corner locations on the image taken by the CCD camera as previously described. Also, the gradients of the projected pixel coordinates are calculated with respect to the extrinsic parameters, Om_k and Tc_k, only, while the initial values of Om_k and Tc_k are used. The errors between the calculated pixel coordinates and the measured pixel coordinates are also calculated, Xk_error = Xk_calculated – Xk_measured. The gradients and Xk_error in combination are used to determine the update increments of the extrinsic parameters, δOm_k and δTc_k. Adding the increments, a new set of extrinsic parameters, Om_k and Tc_k, are obtained. This new set of extrinsic parameters is then used for the next step of the iteration. The iteration continues by calculating the errors, gradients, and upgrading the extrinsic parameters, repeatedly. By minimizing the errors, a final set of extrinsic parameters is obtained. This final set of extrinsic parameters has been obtained by keeping constant a set of known intrinsic parameters, $(c_c, f_c, \alpha_c, k_c)$, through out the iteration.

(3) Knowing the whole set of intrinsic parameters, $(c_c, f_c, \alpha_c, k_c)$, and the extrinsic parameters, Om_k and Tc_k, use the camera model equations, Eqs. 1 – 5, to again calculate a set of projected pixel coordinates, Xk_calculated, of the feature corners from the physical coordinates, X_checkerboard, of the corresponding corner locations on the checkerboard calibration image. Also, the gradients of the projected pixel coordinates with respect to the whole set of intrinsic and extrinsic parameters are calculated.

(4) Compare the calculated pixel coordinates, Xk_calculated, and the measured pixel coordinates, Xk_measured. The measured pixel coordinates were obtained by extracting the corner locations on the image taken by the CCD camera as previously described. The errors between the calculated pixel coordinates and the measured pixel coordinates are evaluated, Xk_error = Xk_calculated – Xk_measured. This is done for each image, k = 1, 2, ..., 10.

(5) The gradients with respect to the intrinsic and extrinsic parameters, as calculated in step (3), and the errors between the calculated pixel coordinates and the measured pixel coordinates, Xk_error, as calculated in step (4), in combination

determine the update increments, (δc_c, δf_c, $\delta \alpha_c$, δk_c; δOm_k, δTc_k) of the intrinsic parameters and the extrinsic parameters. A new set of intrinsic parameters, (c_c, f_c, α_c, k_c), and extrinsic parameters, (Om_k, Tc_k), is obtained after adding the update increments to values of the previous set of intrinsic and extrinsic parameters. Note the difference: the iteration loop in step (2) is for extrinsic parameters only, and the iteration loop in steps (3) to (5) is for intrinsic and extrinsic parameters together.

(6) The fact that the extrinsic factors are independent of the camera intrinsic properties makes the extrinsic parameters somewhat separable from the intrinsic parameters during the optimization process. Holding the intrinsic parameters, (c_c, f_c, α_c, k_c), constant at this moment, an additional iterative process can be performed to refine the extrinsic parameters, (Om_k, Tc_k), to improve values and speed up the convergence of the iterative process. The iterative process used to refine the extrinsic parameters here is the same as the one used in step (2), which only performs iteration on the extrinsic parameters, (Om_k, Tc_k). This additional iteration process is optional; one can choose to use it or not.

(7) If the iterative refining process of step (6) is not used, then the new set of intrinsic parameters and extrinsic parameters as of results of step (5) is used for the next cycle of updating the parameters. If the iterative refining process of step (6) is used, then the set of intrinsic parameters and the refined extrinsic parameters as results of step (6) is used for the next cycle of updating the parameters.

(8) To update the intrinsic and extrinsic parameters, repeat steps (3) to (7). The updating cycle, steps (3) to (7), continues until the errors between the calculated pixel coordinates and the measured pixel coordinates are minimized. Then, the final set of the intrinsic and extrinsic parameters after the iteration is the desired results.

Thus, the camera model is obtained with its intrinsic parameters representing the camera characteristics. The above calibration procedure has been implemented in computer programs to do the numerical calculations. Programs written in MATLAB by J. Y. Bouguet are used in our experiment of the camera calibration for a manufacturing part inspection workstation. However, only part of his program is suitable for use in our application, which is primarily the iterative procedures of retrieving intrinsic and extrinsic parameters. A modification has been made to Bouguet's programs, mainly on the pre-process and post-process of the iterative procedures.

The calibration programs are now ready; next we see how to use them to analyze the experimental data and get the calibration results. In this calibration experiment of a CCD camera used in a manufactured part inspection workstation, the inputs to the calibration programs are the 640 x 480 pixel image data of the checkerboard calibration image pattern placed at various positions and orientations. These image data, as described in section 2, are the ones shown in Figs. A1 to A10. Feature corner locations are extracted from these pixel images using a corner finding program as described in section 3.   Pixel coordinates of the extracted corner locations, in conjunction with grid coordinates of the checkerboard image pattern, then become the immediate inputs to another part of the program which carries out the calculations in the calibration procedure for the camera model containing the intrinsic parameters and extrinsic parameters. Final outputs of the calibration programs are the intrinsic parameters, $(c_c, f_c, \alpha_c, k_c)$, the extrinsic parameters, (Om_k, Tc_k), and the standard deviation error between the measured pixel coordinates and the calculated pixel coordinates using the camera model.

Results of the intrinsic parameters are the following.   Intrinsic parameters are constants to a camera, which are independent of where objects are placed or which images are taken.

$$f_c = [\ 770.7 \quad 768.4\ ] \pm [\ 5.2 \quad 5.1\ ] \qquad \text{pixels}$$
$$c_c = [\ 339.8 \quad 224.3\ ] \pm [\ 2.6 \quad 2.1\ ] \qquad \text{pixels}$$

$$\alpha_c = \quad [\ 0.00030\ ] \pm [\ 0.00035\ ] \qquad\qquad\qquad \text{(Eqs. 12)}$$
$$\Rightarrow \text{angle of pixel axes} = 89.98 \pm 0.02 \text{ degrees}$$

$$k_c = [\ \text{-}0.204 \quad 0.428 \quad \text{-}0.00064 \quad \text{-}0.00218 \quad \text{-}1.278\ ]$$
$$\pm [\ 0.028 \quad 0.277 \quad 0.00059 \quad 0.00069 \quad 0.819\ ]$$

Once the camera model with its parameters is obtained, pixel coordinates on the image plane can be calculated from the corner locations on the checkerboard calibration image using the calibrated camera model, where the calibration image is placed at various positions and orientations.   This set of calculated pixel coordinates is compared to another set of measured pixel coordinates which is obtained by extracting the corner locations from the images taken by the CCD camera.   The errors between the calculated and the measured pixel coordinates indicate the accuracy of the camera model obtained as result of the camera calibration procedure.   The standard deviation of these errors for this experiment determined by the camera calibration program is

$$\text{err} = [\ 0.310 \quad 0.224\ ] \qquad \text{pixel} \qquad\qquad\qquad \text{(Eq. 13)}$$

This indicates that the standard errors as results of this camera calibration procedure are less than one pixel, with the error in x-pixel = 0.310, and in y-pixel = 0.224.

Extrinsic parameters depend on where objects are placed.   Since the checkerboard has been moved to various locations during the calibration, each image taken has a different set of extrinsic parameters associated with it.   As results of this camera calibration procedure, extrinsic parameters, (Om_k, Tc_k), for each of the calibration image, k = 1, 2, ..., 10 , are obtained as shown in Table B11.   With the camera model and extrinsic parameters ready, physical coordinates of the corners of the checkerboard can be re-projected onto each of the pixel images of the checkerboard at various locations.   Because of the error of the camera model, the measurement inaccuracy of physical coordinates and the error in pixel coordinate extraction of the corners, corner re-projection onto each pixel image of the checkerboard has errors associated with it. Fig. 6 shows the corner re-projection error distribution. The corner re-projection errors provide a means to cross check accuracies of the camera model, physical coordinate measurement and pixel coordinate extraction of the corners.

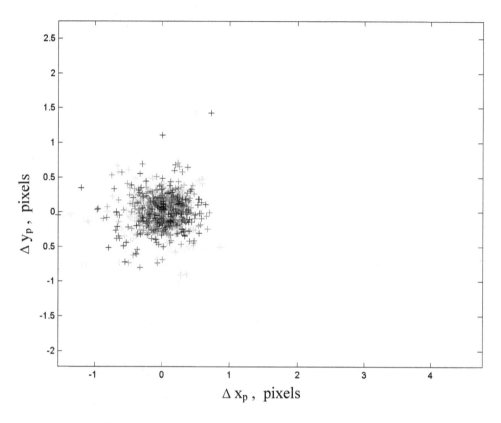

Fig. 6   Corner Re-projection Error Distribution

5. Application of the Camera Model to Measurement of a Machine Part

When a camera takes a picture, the picture contains only a set of planar image values which roughly represent some characteristics of the real objects. There remains uncertainty about what definite objects the camera image represents. The above camera calibration procedure clarifies the uncertainty and provides a clear definition of the relation between the camera image values and the real objects. With quantitative measurement, the picture can be analyzed better. In many applications, the precision of measurement can be very useful and important. Previously, feature information was used in the process of camera calibration. Now, we reverse the process and make use of the camera model to extract information from object features. Because features consist of groups of large numbers of points, a variety of properties can be derived from the feature information. Some example properties are the distinguishable characteristics and global locations of features. Global locations of features are just the position and orientation of an object if all the features are fixed on one object.

To see how to use a camera to find out where the objects' positions and orientations are, use the optimization algorithm in the calibration procedure to find the rotation vector and the translation vector of the objects. To see how accurately a camera can identify features of objects from their images, use the camera model to calculate the image pixel coordinates of the features on the objects from the known object geometry, and then compare the calculated pixel coordinates of the feature locations on the objects with the pixel coordinates of the corresponding feature locations on the images taken by the camera. Object geometry can be obtained by tape measuring the object, or from a CAD (Computer Aided Design) model of the object (Fig. 7).

Let's look more closely into the detailed process of using a camera to do the measurement of features and object locations. The key to camera imaging measurement is the location of feature points on an object. Feature point locations contain both information of the relative positions of the feature points and that of the positions and orientations of the object due to its gross motion. When the camera takes an image of the object, feature point locations on the object are converted to feature point locations in the image. This conversion is done in the camera model through the intrinsic parameters and the extrinsic parameters. After the camera is calibrated, the intrinsic parameters in the camera model become known, and the conversion between feature point locations on the object and the feature point locations in the image becomes definite and comes to a one to one direct correspondence by using the formulation of the camera model. Thereafter, one only needs to work on the feature point locations in the image to find out exactly what's going on with the object. Previously during the camera calibration process, feature point locations both in the image and on the object were known, and they were used to find the intrinsic and extrinsic parameters in the camera model. Now, in the measurement application of the calibrated camera, point locations of features in the image are still the known quantity, but point locations of features on the object become the unknown. And we need to have a procedure to find the feature point locations on the object.

5.1   Finding the Object Location

The camera recognizes feature point locations of the object in a stationary camera coordinate frame. Features are attached to the object coordinate frame and move with the object. While features are stationary with respect to the object coordinate frame, the object moves in translational and rotational ways with respect to the camera coordinate frame. Therefore, the object's location is defined by its translation and rotation with respect to the camera coordinate frame. This means to find the object location is to find the translation and rotation of the object's motion with respect to the camera coordinate frame. Feature point locations with respect to the object are of real interest in the final application, but sometimes the object location is also of interest. The known quantity now is the feature point locations with respect to the camera coordinate frame. Given a sufficient number of feature point locations in the object coordinate frame and their locations in camera coordinate frame measured by the camera, the object's location can be resolved from the camera model. In practice, the accuracy of the resulting object location depends much on the camera resolution and the size of relative positions of the feature points used.

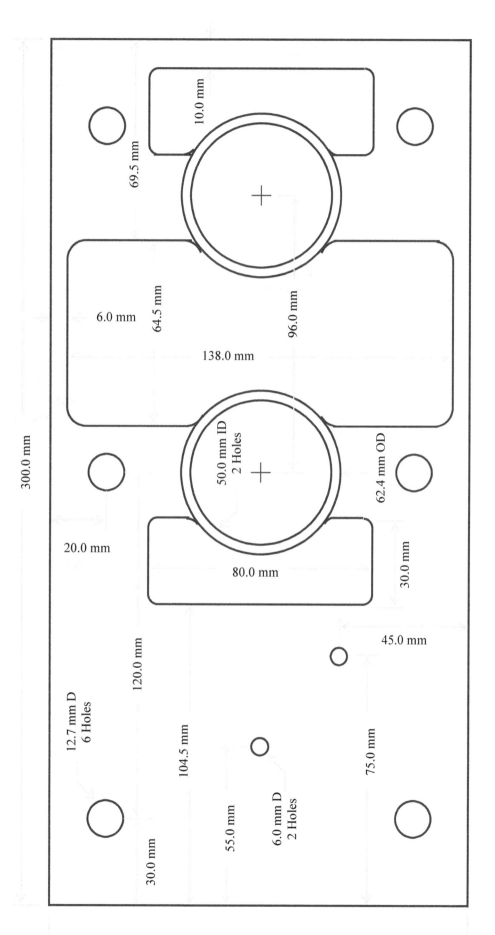

Fig. 7   CAD Drawing of the Machine Part Specimen

19

The precise quantitative measure of a feature in an image is the pixel coordinates of the feature point locations. These pixel coordinates are the raw data of the camera imaging measurement, and they are used in the following analysis to find out information about an object's geometry and its location. To begin with, physical coordinates of the feature point locations in the camera coordinate frame are back-calculated from the pixel coordinates by using the camera model. However, at this time, the feature coordinates in the camera frame do not have 3D information yet. The other component, the z-component, needs to come from information about the object location with respect to camera frame. When the camera took a picture of the object, there was a 3D to 2D projection which transformed the 3D object geometry into 2D pixel coordinates of image features. Now, we need a 2D to 3D back-projection to find coordinates of the geometrical features in the object coordinate frame. But the object's location needs to be found first. A set of feature points with coordinates known in both the camera coordinate frame and the object coordinate frame are all that is needed to determine the object location. The 2D to 3D back-projection coupled with the translational and rotational transformation of the object's rigid body motion requires an iterative procedure to solve for the object position and orientation with respect to the camera coordinate frame. The algorithm described in step (2) of the camera calibration procedure can be used for the iterative resolution of object location. However, while in the calibration procedure features used were corners of the checkerboard calibration pattern, they should be replaced by the selected object features used now to locate the object. Step (2) of the camera calibration procedure extracts the extrinsic parameters of the camera model when the intrinsic parameters of the camera model are known. These extrinsic parameters contain a rotation vector and a translation vector, which represent the rotational and translational rigid body motion of the object, respectively.

5.2 Verifying the Camera Model

Once the position and orientation of an object relative to the camera are determined from pixel coordinates of the point locations of a few selected features and their corresponding physical coordinates, pixel coordinates of many other features can be calculated from their corresponding physical coordinates on the object. Comparison can then be made between the measured pixel coordinates of features and the calculated pixel coordinates of the same features. Measured pixel coordinates are the ones determined from the features on the image of the object. Calculated pixel coordinates are the ones calculated from the feature point locations on the object using the calibrated camera model. This comparison will show how good the matching accuracy is between the feature coordinates measured by the camera and those predicted by the camera model. However, the camera measurement only provides 2D coordinates. Information on the depth dimension has to come from an assumption that the features lie on a surface. Otherwise, it has to come from multiple images with the camera being placed at two or more different locations. In this experiment, we assume all the features of interest lie in one plane, and one camera location is used, but the plane can be placed at any 3D position and orientation.

5.3 Example Calculation

As an example to verify the accuracy of the calibrated camera model, a manufactured machine part is chosen as the test specimen to demonstrate the application of the camera model on the measurement of object geometry using a CCD camera. First, an image of the machine part is taken as shown in Fig. C1 (see Appendix C), which is at a negative tilt 24.0° position. An edge detection computer program using the Sobel method implemented in MATLAB is then used to extract edge features on the machine part image.   These extracted edges of the machine part are shown in Fig. C3.   The extreme four corners, which are at the intersections of the outer four edges, are chosen as the set of feature point locations used for the determination of position and orientation of the machine part.   The physical coordinates of the four corners were measured with a ruler and they are

$$
\begin{aligned}
(XX_o\text{corner1}, YY_o\text{corner1}, ZZ_o\text{corner1}) &= (\ 0.0,\ 0.0,\ 0.0\ ) && \text{mm} \\
(XX_o\text{corner2}, YY_o\text{corner2}, ZZ_o\text{corner2}) &= (\ 0.0,\ 149.4,\ 0.0\ ) && \text{mm} \\
(XX_o\text{corner3}, YY_o\text{corner3}, ZZ_o\text{corner3}) &= (\ 299.2,\ 149.4,\ 0.0\ ) && \text{mm} \\
(XX_o\text{corner4}, YY_o\text{corner4}, ZZ_o\text{corner4}) &= (\ 299.2,\ 0.0,\ 0.0\ ) && \text{mm}
\end{aligned}
\qquad \text{(Eqs. 14)}
$$

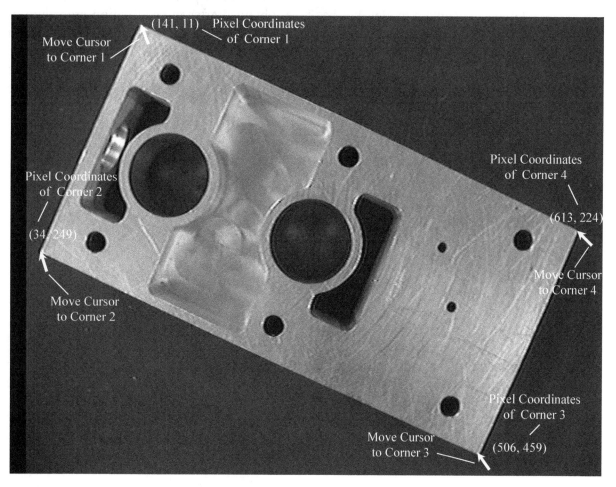

Fig. 8   Move the Cursor to Four Corners of the Machine Part Image
and Read the Pixel Coordinates of Each Corner

A MATLAB image GUI (Graphical User Interface) program was written to pick up the pixel coordinates of the four corners from the camera image of the machine part in Fig. C1. The GUI allows a user to move the cursor across the machine part image and displays the pixel coordinates of any point the cursor reaches. Visual judgement decides whether the position of a corner matches the cursor position. When the cursor matches a corner, the pixel coordinates of that corner are picked from program outputs. Pixel coordinates of all four corners on the machine part image are thus picked (Fig. 8). Further refined pixel coordinates of the four corners can be obtained by zooming into each corner and interpolating neighboring pixels to get the best estimates. These best estimates are listed in the following.

$$
\begin{aligned}
(Xcorner1, Ycorner1) &= (\ 140.6, \quad 11.0\ ) \quad &&\text{pixels} \\
(Xcorner2, Ycorner2) &= (\ 34.2, \quad 248.7\ ) \quad &&\text{pixels} \\
(Xcorner3, Ycorner3) &= (\ 506.5, \quad 459.3\ ) \quad &&\text{pixels} \\
(Xcorner4, Ycorner4) &= (\ 612.9, \quad 224.2\ ) \quad &&\text{pixels}
\end{aligned}
\qquad \text{(Eqs. 15)}
$$

Once the positions of the four corners are measured both in pixel coordinates and physical coordinates, the relative position and orientation of the machine part with respect to the camera are fixed. Given the camera model that has been obtained after the calibration procedure of Section 4, and its intrinsic parameters known as in Eqs. 12, the extrinsic parameter extraction program as described before can be used to find relative position and orientation of the machine part with respect to the camera. As the results, the position and orientation of the machine part are expressed as a translation vector and a rotation vector, respectively, in the following:

$$
\begin{aligned}
Tc\_machine\text{-}part &= (\ -114.4,\ -122.5,\ 431.9\ ) \quad &&\text{mm} \\
Om\_machine\text{-}part &= (\ -0.000803,\ -0.0133,\ 0.423\ ) \quad &&\text{radians}
\end{aligned}
$$

$$
Rc\_machine\text{-}part =
\begin{bmatrix}
0.912 & -0.411 & -0.0128 \\
0.410 & 0.912 & -0.00355 \\
0.0131 & -0.00199 & 0.999
\end{bmatrix}
\qquad \text{(Eqs. 16)}
$$

$$
err\_machine\text{-}part = [\ 0.402 \quad 0.720\ ] \qquad \text{pixel} \qquad \text{(Eq. 17)}
$$

A second image of the same machine part specimen is taken (Fig. C2), but this time the specimen is rotated clockwise to a new position at a positive tilt of 25.4° . The Sobel edge detection method [9,10,11] is also applied to the second image, and the edges are found as shown in Fig. C4. The same procedures to determine the pixel coordinates of the four corners and to find the relative position and orientation of the machine part with respect to the camera are applied to the second image, and the results are the following:

$$(Xcorner1, Ycorner1) = (620.6, \quad 242.3) \quad \text{pixels}$$
$$(Xcorner2, Ycorner2) = (509.0, \quad 7.8) \quad \text{pixels}$$
$$(Xcorner3, Ycorner3) = (40.6, \quad 233.9) \quad \text{pixels}$$
$$(Xcorner4, Ycorner4) = (154.8, \quad 466.4) \quad \text{pixels}$$

(Eqs. 18)

$$Tc\_machine\text{-}part = (162.4, \quad 10.2, \quad 433.4) \qquad \text{mm}$$
$$Om\_machine\text{-}part = (-0.00134, \quad -0.0143, \quad 2.69) \qquad \text{radians}$$

$$Rc\_machine\text{-}part = \begin{bmatrix} -0.900 & -0.435 & -0.00326 \\ 0.435 & -0.900 & -0.00988 \\ -0.00136 & -0.0103 & 0.999 \end{bmatrix}$$

(Eqs. 19)

$$err\_machine\text{-}part = [\, 0.274 \quad 0.540 \,] \qquad \text{pixel}$$

(Eq. 20)

Knowing the camera model with its intrinsic parameters, and also knowing the extrinsic parameters which represent the position and orientation of the machine part with respect to the camera, pixel coordinates of the point locations of all the features on the machine part can now be calculated from the physical coordinates of the feature locations using the camera model.

A set of features on the machine part is selected, which consists of circular edges of several holes and the four line edges of the outer boundary. Pixel coordinates of this set of features are calculated using the calibrated camera model obtained above with its intrinsic parameters given in Eqs. 12 and the extrinsic parameters currently determined for the machine part in its two positions. Then, this set of calculated pixel coordinates of the selected features on the machine part is superimposed onto each of the camera images of the machine part, as shown in Figs. C5 – C6. As can be seen from Figs. C5 – C6, the calculated pixel coordinates of the selected features fit in quite well over all with those on the camera image of the machine part. The positioning accuracy of the calculated pixel coordinates on the camera image is on the order of 1 mm in the center portion and 2 mm in the outer portion. This positioning accuracy may depend on the focal length of the camera, and on the accuracy in the determination of the pixel coordinates of the four corners, etc. as discussed in the following error analyses. For comparison of the positioning error with the total dimension, the length of the specimen is 299.2 mm, and the width is 149.4 mm. The machine part is placed at a distance of approximately 45 cm from the camera.

6. Variations of Center Position of Calibration Data Sample and Error Analyses

Depending on the locations of the object being viewed by the camera, the camera model as defined in Eq. 5 may fit well or not. The camera may have different properties at different locations, $P_c = (X_c, Y_c, Z_c)$, where (X_c, Y_c, Z_c) are coordinates of the location P_c with respect to the camera reference frame. This means that the functional relationships described by the camera model may vary for different locations.   Besides, even if the same functional relationship can be used, the intrinsic parameters in the camera model may vary for different locations.   Therefore, the calibration images used to obtain the camera model need to be placed within a localized region around a center point, P_c, in the camera reference frame.   This non-uniformity of the camera properties across the camera reference frame contributes to the major source of error and inaccuracy in the camera calibration procedure.   If one tries to model the camera imaging transformation with a single camera model over a large region in the camera reference frame, errors and inaccuracy of the resulting model may be too large for practical use.   To model the camera imaging transformation over a large region, many camera models may be used together, each having different intrinsic parameters.

In the application of the calibrated camera model to determine the positions and orientations of the machine part, two other sources of error are important.   One is the error in the pixel coordinates of the four corners of the part as determined by extracting their pixel positions from the part image.   The other is the error in the measurement of the physical coordinates of the same four corners of the machine part.   In this current experiment, the error in measurement of the physical coordinates of the four corners of the machine part is about 0.5 mm.   Error in determining the pixel coordinates of the four corners of the machine part from its camera image is about 1 or 2 pixels.   In pixel coordinates, the length of the machine part is 517.1 pixels and the width 258.1 pixels.   With the known length and width in physical coordinates as given in section 5, this yields the unit conversion factor between the pixel coordinates and the physical coordinates to be 0.5786 mm/pixel.   The error of 1 or 2 pixels in the pixel coordinates of the part corners is then about 0.6 mm to 1.2 mm.

As viewed from the superimposed picture of each machine part image and the feature point locations calculated from the CAD model (Figs. C5 – C6), the error between the feature locations on the image and the calculated feature locations is about 1 mm in the center portion of the part image and about 2 mm in the outer portion of the image.   This error between the feature locations as they appear in the image and the calculated feature locations may reasonably be interpreted as due to the combination of the 0.5 mm error in the measurement of physical coordinates of the part corners, the 0.6 mm to 1.2 mm error in the pixel coordinates of the part corners extracted from the image, and possibly also the non-uniformity of the calibrated camera model across the camera reference frame.   That is, the error between the feature locations on the image and the feature locations obtained from model calculation is consistent with the consequences of the three error sources listed above.

The 0.5 mm uncertainty we have when using a ruler for the measurement of physical coordinates of the machine part corners is considered quite large compared to the uncertainty achieved by other commonly used dimensional measurement tools.   For example, a typical digital caliper will routinely measure to 0.01 mm accuracy or better.   However, a ruler is easily accessible. Using a ruler to do dimensional measurement is the simplest and fastest way compared to other possiblilities.   As a first trial with a camera calibration procedure, we use a ruler and it is sufficient for our current purpose. Our purpose in this experiment focuses on the demonstration of the procedure of applying a calibrated camera to measure the geometry of a machine part rather than on the accuracy of the geometry itself. After this first trial, many improvements can be done to achieve higher accuracy; that is, other high precision methods in measuring physical coordinates can be pursued when it is necessary.

6.1 Errors in the Calibration Process

A camera imaging system has errors. To find out how much error is in a camera imaging system, a calibration was done. However, the calibration process itself has errors. Calibration introduces new errors adding to the error of the camera imaging system. A camera imaging probe converts the geometry of an object into a camera image. As a way of quantitative measurement, object geometry is characterized with sets of feature points. The camera image conversion transforms geometrical features of the object into image features. Measuring the physical coordinates of the feature points of object geometry and the image coordinates of the image feature points will quantitatively define the performance and characteristics of the camera probe. In the calibration process, we call the coordinates measured from the physical feature points the measured physical coordinates, and those measured form the image feature points the measured image coordinates. Any measurement has error, therefore measured physical coordinates have error and measured image coordinates have error. For the purpose of calibration and performance verification of a camera imaging measurement system, measured physical coordinates must be obtained from measurement tools other than the camera probe itself. Measured image coordinates are the pixel coordinates of the image feature points registered by the CCD image detector array.

The transformation property of the camera conversion of object geometrical features into image features is represented by a camera model. However, the camera model is only an approximation to the camera image transformation because of the limit number of parameters used in the model formulation. Thus, the camera model naturally has error in itself. A camera model is obtained through calibration process using known values of pixel coordinates and measured physical coordinates of calibration patterns. Since both pixel coordinates and measured physical coordinates have errors, the calibrated camera model will have error due to them in addition to the inherent error due to the approximation in model formulation.

Pixel coordinates are obtained in two major steps after the camera image is formed. First, the camera image is registered into pixels by the CCD detector array and forms the pixel image. Then, pixel coordinates of feature points of interest are extracted from features in the pixel image. Pixel coordinate error mostly comes from feature extraction error. The error due to image registration into pixels normally is much smaller than feature extraction error. Camera imaging conversion causes images to smear, blur and distort. This causes confusion in the followup feature extraction process. The discretization of the registration process of converting the image coordinates to pixel coordinates causes fine features to change shape. Feature information finer than a pixel is lost.

Error associated with the measured physical coordinates comes from the error in the measurement system or tools used. In the case of current camera calibration, the measurement system or tools obviously should be a system other than the camera imaging probe itself. Depending on the measurement system or tools available, the error of the measured physical coordinates can be large or small. For the purpose of camera calibration, a measurement tool that would result in an error of the measured physical coordinates smaller than the errors associated with the pixel coordinates and the camera model is preferred.

6.2 Errors in the Inter-relations among Camera Calibration, Locating Objects and Feature Matching

To prepare the camera imaging system for the measurement of object geometry, three things were done: camera model calibration, object location calibration, and verification of feature matching accuracy. Each of these three stages used a different camera imaging target. In camera model calibration, the imaging target used is called a camera model calibration pattern. In object location calibration, the imaging target used is an object location calibration frame. In the verification of feature matching accuracy, the imaging target used is the object geometry features. The relation between pixel coordinates and physical coordinates of the feature points on the camera model calibration pattern yields the camera model. The relation between pixel coordinates and physical coordinates of the feature points on the object location calibration frame locates the object's position and orientation with respect to the camera. When a camera imaging system is applied to measure the geometry of an object, its performance is evaluated by the matching accuracy between the pixel coordinates of the extracted feature points from an object's image and the physical coordinates of the corresponding feature points on the object. After calibration of the camera imaging system, we have conducted two tests to verify the feature matching accuracy. The matching accuracy is the error obtained by subtracting the projection of physical coordinates from the pixel coordinates.

Before doing object location calibration, a camera model must already exist. Before doing feature matching verification, the object location must already be calibrated and a camera model must already exist. The accuracy of the camera model depends on the accuracy of pixel coordinates of the feature points extracted from image of the calibration pattern and the accuracy of physical coordinates of the calibration pattern. The accuracy of the object location calibration depends on the accuracy of pixel coordinates of the feature points extracted from the object location calibration frame, the accuracy of physical coordinates of the object location calibration frame, and the accuracy of the camera model. The matching accuracy between the pixel coordinates of the object geometry image features and the physical coordinates of the object geometry features depends on the accuracy of pixel coordinates of the feature points extracted from image of the object, the accuracy of physical coordinates of the object geometry features, the accuracy of the object location calibration, and the accuracy of the camera model.

The results of this experiment have shown: (1) With the symmetric property of the checkerboard calibration pattern, the physical coordinates of its corners are easily determined with precision and their pixel coordinates can also be extracted from the image of the checkerboard with precision. Thus, the camera model is calibrated with a sub-pixel accuracy. (2) With an object location calibration frame chosen to be the rectangle of the outer boundary of a machine part, the four corners of the machine part are chosen to be the key points used to calibrate the position and orientation of the object. Physical coordinates of the machine part four corners are measured with an accuracy of 0.5 mm / 299.2 mm = 0.167 % in length and 0.5 mm / 149.4 mm = 0.335 % in width. With an optimization procedure and a zooming procedure applied to the identification of the corner pixels, pixel coordinates of the machine part corners are extracted from the machine part image with an accuracy of 1 to 2 pixels / 517.1 pixels ($\approx$ 0.193 % to 0.387 %) in length and 1 to 2 pixels / 258.1 pixels ($\approx$ 0.387% to 0.775 %) in width. This also results in a sub-pixel accuracy for the object location calibration. However, the error for this object location calibration is larger than the error for the camera model calibration. (3) With easily available measurement tools, the physical coordinates of feature points of the object geometry have been measured with an accuracy of about 0.5 mm. Using the camera model and the calibrated object coordinate frame, the physical coordinates of the geometry feature points on the object were back-projected onto the image of the object to match the pixel coordinates of the corresponding feature points in the image. As a result, the matching accuracy between the pixel coordinates and the physical coordinates of the feature points is determined to be about 1 mm to 2 mm ($\approx$ 2 to 4 pixels) throughout different regions of the image. This matching accuracy is an indicator of how accurately the camera probe can be applied to measure object feature geometry.

The ability to accurately measure the physical coordinates of the object geometry and accurately extract pixel coordinates from image features is an important factor that affects the camera model calibration accuracy, the object location calibration accuracy and the verification accuracy for matching the back-projection image of object geometry using the camera model with the direct camera image of the object geometry. If the accuracies of measured physical coordinates and pixel coordinates of the corners of the camera model calibration image pattern are improved, then the camera model calibration accuracy can be further refined, the subsequent object location calibration accuracy and the verification accuracy of matching physical coordinates of object feature points wth their pixel coordinates can also be improved. If the accuracies of the measured physical coordinates and pixel coordinates of the key points in the object location calibration frame can be improved, then the object location calibration accuracy can be further refined and the verification accuracy of matching physical coordinates of object feature points with their pixel coordinates can also be improved. Lastly, if the accuracies of measured physical coordinates and pixel coordinates of the object feature points can be improved significantly, then it is possible that sub-pixel accuracy in matching the back-projection image of object geometry using the camera model with the direct camera image of the object geometry can also be obtained to verify the applicability of the camera imaging technique in measuring object geometry.

6.3 Tracing Error Propagation among Various Stages of Image Transformation

The exact inter-relationships among the errors associated with the camera model calibration, object location calibration, and the verification of the feature matching accuracy can be seen from the camera imaging transformation formula, Eq. 5. The camera model contains intrinsic parameters, (f_c, c_c, α_c, k_c), as Eqs. 1 - 4; and extrinsic parameters, (Rc, Tc), as in Eq. 7. The camera model transforms the physical coordinates, (X_c, Y_c, Z_c), of feature points on the object into pixel coordinates, (x_p, y_p), of the feature points in the image. Camera model calibration procedure determines the camera characteristic values, (f_c, c_c, α_c, k_c). Object location calibration procedure determines the object's position and orientation, (Rc, Tc), with respect to the camera. Camera model calibration has been done to our camera imaging system with the calibrated values of (f_c, c_c, α_c, k_c) shown in Eq. 12. Errors associated with the camera model result in a sub-pixel accuracy (Eq. 13) as of the camera model calibration. Object location calibration has been conducted for two test cases as described in section 5.3. For each of the two test cases, the relative position and orientation, (Rc, Tc) in Eqs. 16 or 19, of the object is determined by matching the physical coordinates, (Eqs. 14), of the four corners of the object with their respective pixel coordinates, (Eqs. 15 or 18) in the camera image. As can be seen from above error analyses, our accuracy in measurement of (X_c, Y_c, Z_c) of the machine part four corners is about 0.5 mm, and that for (x_p, y_p) of the four corners is $\approx$ 1 to 2 pixels. These consequently also result in a sub-pixel accuracy (Eq. 17 or 20) for locating the object position and orientation. However, this object position and orientation accuracy is lower than the camera calibration accuracy (Eq. 13).

In doing camera model calibration, (X_c, Y_c, Z_c) and (x_p, y_p) of key points in the calibration pattern are the inputs to the camera imaging transformation formula, and the camera characteristic values, $(f_c, c_c, \alpha_c, k_c)$, are the output results. In doing object location calibration, (X_c, Y_c, Z_c) and (x_p, y_p) of key points in the object location calibration frame are the inputs, and the object position and orientation, (Rc, Tc) are the output results. Whereas in the case of object geometry measurement, (x_p, y_p) of feature points in an object image and the camera model parameters, $\{(f_c, c_c, \alpha_c, k_c), (Rc, Tc)\}$, are the inputs; and (X'_c, Y'_c, Z'_c) of geometry feature points on the object are the desired outputs. We need to notice that (X'_c, Y'_c, Z'_c) have a different meaning from (X_c, Y_c, Z_c). The forward-projected physical coordinates, (X'_c, Y'_c, Z'_c), are obtained by projecting the camera measured pixel coordinates, (x_p, y_p), through the use of the camera model transformation, $\{(f_c, c_c, \alpha_c, k_c), (Rc, Tc)\}$, into physical coordinate space. Yet, in the other case where we verify the accuracy of using the camera imaging system to do the object geometry measurement, a set of back-projected pixel coordinates, (x'_p, y'_p), calculated from the physical coordinates, (X_c, Y_c, Z_c), of geometry feature points on an object is overlaid onto the set of pixel coordinates, (x_p, y_p), of corresponding image feature points. In this accuracy verification case, (X_c, Y_c, Z_c) of geometry feature points on the object and the camera model parameters, $\{(f_c, c_c, \alpha_c, k_c), (Rc, Tc)\}$, are the inputs to the camera imaging transformation formula; and the back-projected pixel coordinates, (x'_p, y'_p), are the outputs. In all cases, errors associated with the inputs add and multiply each other, and result in the errors associated with the outputs.

The matching error of 2 to 4 pixels shown in the overlaid pictures, Figs. C5-C6, between (x_p, y_p) and (x'_p, y'_p) of the object geometry feature points indicates that the object geometry measurement error is too high for certain direct use of the camera probe. So, under what situations would the object geometry measurement error be reduced to the same level as the camera calibration error in the sub-pixel range? Let us examine some possibilities. But, first we look into more details about the error scenarios of object geometry measurement. The pixel coordinates, (x_p, y_p), of the geometry feature points may grossly represent two meanings: one we denote as $(x_p, y_p)_{raw}$, the other $(x_p, y_p)_{extracted}$. In the image data stream, $(x_p, y_p)_{raw}$ are the pixel coordinates of feature points immediately after pixel registration of the feature images by the CCD array detector, whereas $(x_p, y_p)_{extracted}$ are the pixel coordinates after feature extraction process of the image features. In object geometry measurement, if it refers to the measurement of $(x_p, y_p)_{raw}$, then we call it raw image measurement. If it refers to the measurement of $(x_p, y_p)_{extracted}$, then we call it feature extraction measurement. Feature extraction process of $(x_p, y_p)_{extracted}$ from $(x_p, y_p)_{raw}$ introduces some feature extraction error.

Thus, $(x_p, y_p)_{extracted}$ equals $(x_p, y_p)_{raw}$ plus the feature extraction error. In the two test cases of measuring machine part geometry, the feature extraction error is estimated to be 2 to 3 pixels.

After the raw image measurement, $(x_p, y_p)_{raw}$ are transformed into the projected physical coordinates, $(X'_c, Y'_c, Z'_c)_{raw}$, by the camera model, $\{(f_c, c_c, \alpha_c, k_c), (Rc, Tc)\}$. And, $(x_p, y_p)_{extracted}$ are transformed into the projected physical coordinates, $(X'_c, Y'_c, Z'_c)_{extracted}$. We then refer the accuracy of raw image measurement of object geometry as the accuracy associated with $(X'_c, Y'_c, Z'_c)_{raw}$, and the accuracy of feature extraction measurement of object geometry as the accuracy associated with $(X'_c, Y'_c, Z'_c)_{extracted}$. The error associated with $(X'_c, Y'_c, Z'_c)_{raw}$ is a combination of the error associated with $(x_p, y_p)_{raw}$ and the error associated with the camera model, $\{(f_c, c_c, \alpha_c, k_c), (Rc, Tc)\}$. Similarly, the error associated with $(X'_c, Y'_c, Z'_c)_{extracted}$ is a combination of the error associated with $(x_p, y_p)_{extracted}$ and the error associated with the camera model.

Now, let us consider a case in which the position and orientation of the object relative to the camera are precisely known from some source. That is, in this case we assume that the error associated with (Rc, Tc) is zero. Then, the only remaining error source in the camera imaging transformation is the error associated with the intrinsic parameters, $(f_c, c_c, \alpha_c, k_c)$. Therefore, in this case the accuracy of $(X'_c, Y'_c, Z'_c)_{raw}$ would be the same as that for the camera calibration, which is a sub-pixel accuracy. With the sub-pixel error of $(f_c, c_c, \alpha_c, k_c)$ and the estimated 2 to 3 pixel error in feature extraction, the accuracy of $(X'_c, Y'_c, Z'_c)_{extracted}$ is estimated to be 2 to 3 pixels. If error for the feature extraction of object geometry can be made zero, then $(X'_c, Y'_c, Z'_c)_{extracted} = (X'_c, Y'_c, Z'_c)_{raw}$ and the accuracy of $(X'_c, Y'_c, Z'_c)_{extracted}$ is also sub-pixel.

In reality, it is not possible to have zero error in (Rc, Tc). Our object location calibration in this experiment gives us the actual errors of (Rc, Tc) in the sub-pixel range, see Eq.17 or 20, somewhat higher than the camera model calibration error. For this real case, $(X'_c, Y'_c, Z'_c)_{raw}$ has an accuracy about the same as the sub-pixel accuracy after object location calibration. And, the error of $(X'_c, Y'_c, Z'_c)_{extracted}$ is estimated to be somewhat larger than 2 to 3 pixels.

Object geometry measurement using a camera imaging system yields (x_p, y_p) in image coordinate space and (X'_c, Y'_c, Z'_c) in forward-projected physical coordinate space. By error analyses on the imaging measurement system, we know approximately what the accuracy of (x_p, y_p) or (X'_c, Y'_c, Z'_c) is. But, to know for certain what the accuracy of (x_p, y_p) or (X'_c, Y'_c, Z'_c) really is, we verify it with the object geometry measurement of (X_c, Y_c, Z_c) using other types of tool. The verification is done by matching (x_p, y_p) with (x'_p, y'_p), or by matching (X'_c, Y'_c, Z'_c) with (X_c, Y_c, Z_c). In this experiment, we match (x_p, y_p) with (x'_p, y'_p) to verify our object geometry measurement accuracy using the camera probe, as demonstrated by Figs. C5-C6.

In an ideal case in which true physical coordinates, $(X_c, Y_c, Z_c)_{true}$, of the feature geometry are available, we match (x_p, y_p) with the back-projected $(x'_p, y'_p)_{true}$ of $(X_c, Y_c, Z_c)_{true}$ to verify the accuracy of object geometry measurement. By true physical coordinates we mean the physical coordinates of object features are known to be exactly precise without error; they are the actual dimensions of the object geometry. In this case, the matching accuracy between (x_p, y_p) and $(x'_p, y'_p)_{true}$ becomes the accuracy of object geometry measurement itself. That is, the matching accuracy between $(x_p, y_p)_{raw}$ and $(x'_p, y'_p)_{true}$ is the sub-pixel accuracy after object location calibration. And, the matching accuracy between $(x_p, y_p)_{extracted}$ and $(x'_p, y'_p)_{true}$ is the estimated 2 to 3 pixels.

Usually, the physical coordinates of the feature geometry of a machine part are known through physical measurements on the object using various tools, and we call these the measured physical coordinates, $(X_c, Y_c, Z_c)_{measured}$. One can also obtain knowledge of the physical coordinates of feature geometry of the machine part by reference to its CAD model. Because the machine part is manufactured according to a CAD model, its dimensions must be close to the designed values specified by the CAD model – within the accuracy of the manufacturing technology used. In our error analyses here, we call these values the CAD model values of physical coordinates of the machine part feature geometry. Due to the coordinate measurement error, measured physical coordinates always differ from the true physical coordinates. Due to manufacturing error, CAD model values of the physical coordinates also differ from the true physical coordinates.

A criterion used to claim the accuracy of the camera imaging probe in measuring the feature geometry of an object is to compare the pixel coordinates of the features with the physical coordinates of the same features. When the true physical coordinates of features are available, we compare the pixel coordinates with them and call the difference the true accuracy of the probe in measuring object feature geometry. Most of the time, the true physical coordinates are not available. Then, we verify the accuracy by comparing the pixel coordinates of object features with a set of reference values, $(X_c, Y_c, Z_c)_{reference}$, of the physical coordinates of the same features. This set of reference values can be the measured physical coordinates or CAD model values, or a combination of the two. When the pixel coordinates are compared with the reference values of physical coordinates, we call the difference the relative accuracy of the probe in measuring object feature geometry. More precisely, in the pixel coordinate space the true accuracy is the matching accuracy between (x_p, y_p) and $(x'_p, y'_p)_{true}$. And, the relative accuracy is the matching accuracy between (x_p, y_p) and the back-projected $(x'_p, y'_p)_{reference}$ of $(X_c, Y_c, Z_c)_{reference}$. In this experiment, the matching accuracy between $(x_p, y_p)_{raw}$ and $(x'_p, y'_p)_{reference}$ is about 1 pixel due to the estimated 0.5 mm error in $(X_c, Y_c, Z_c)_{reference}$. And, the matching accuracy between $(x_p, y_p)_{extracted}$ and $(x'_p, y'_p)_{reference}$ is the 2 to 4 pixels shown in Figs. C5-C6. If the measured physical coordinates can be made close to the true physical coordinates by using some precise measurement method or the CAD model values can be made close to the true physical coordinates by precisely manufacturing the part, then it is possible that the relative accuracy can be made close to the true accuracy.

7. Comparisons With Other Dimensional Measurement Methods

Camera imaging systems use optical properties between the sensors and the target objects to do measurement. Proper optics designs are likely to suit the various special requirements of different measurement environments. The range of measurement can be large as for satellite remote sensing, small as for medical imaging, and even of molecular scale. Measurement accuracy varies from the optical resolution of feature geometry to the order of a wavelength. CCD cameras employ pixel arrays of optical sensing units and do two-dimensional measurement simultaneously. Beside the potential of increasing measurement accuracy, the CCD camera imaging measurement technique has the advantage of recognizing object features. It is also a non-contact, non-intrusive and non-destructive measurement technique. All these factors make the CCD camera imaging measurement technique a potential candidate for high precision, object feature recognizing measurement in manufacturing metrology.

The accuracy of measurements using the CCD camera imaging technique depends on the pixel resolution of the CCD sensors, the amplification factor of the lenses, and the imaging resolution of the lenses. For the camera setup used in this experiment, a positioning accuracy of about 1 mm to 2 mm has been obtained as the result of a test of locating feature points on a machine part using a calibrated CCD camera. If lenses with larger amplification factors are used, the measurement accuracy using the CCD camera imaging technique is expected to be better than 1 mm, with the current setup for machine part feature identification.

Dimensional measurement using a laser interferometer has a very high accuracy better than 1 μm. It also has a very long range of measurement, more than 10 meters. Typical coordinate measuring machines (CMM) have measurement accuracy of about 0.0025 mm and measurement range of about 1 meter. Acoustic sensors used in linear position measurement have accuracy on the order of 1 mm.

Compared with the accuracy of laser interferometer measurement, the measurement technique using a CCD camera imaging system is far less accurate unless high amplification lenses are added to the camera. However, the laser interferometer requires a retro-reflecting mirror attached to the end point of measurement, which prevents direct measurement of the feature geometry of an object. The pixel array on the CCD sensor surface makes it possible to directly measure the feature geometry of an object, and this becomes a big advantage of CCD camera imaging measurements over laser interferometer measurements.

The basic limitation of the measurement accuracy of a CCD camera is the pixel resolution of the CCD sensor. From the error analysis above, if a careful camera calibration procedure is conducted with precise measurement of the pixel coordinates and the physical coordinates of feature point locations of a calibration target, maybe it is provable through more experiments in the future that sub-pixel measurement accuracy can be attained with the CCD camera imaging measurement technique. Depending on the amplification factor of the lenses used with camera, this sub-pixel accuracy may be translated into various degrees of accuracy in the real physical dimension of the objects being measured. From the test results of current experiment for machine part feature measurement, estimation can be extended to other general cases of using camera imaging technique for object geometry measurement. For a simple lens assembly, typical measurement accuracy with a CCD camera in real physical dimension is about 1 mm or better. Combined with high amplification optical lenses, the CCD camera measurement accuracy can possibly be improved to far better than 1 mm in real physical dimension. Again, this still needs further experimental verification.

8. Future Work on Improving Camera Imaging Measurement

The entire problem of using camera imaging measurement technique to map the geometry of machine parts is very complex. To get high accuracy and complete mapping of complicated object geometry is rather difficult in many instances. However, in practical applications, high accuracy measurement uniformly across the object surface and complete geometry mapping may not be necessary. Selected regions of geometry mapping and variable ranges of measurement accuracy are often sufficient for a particular application. For optimum results and efficiency required, measurement procedures may vary and depend a lot on the geometrical configuration of the objects and the sensing camera. In a way, the versatility of meeting various needs makes camera imaging measurement technique useful. Nevertheless, measurement accuracy is still the goal to pursue for this developing technology.

Every measurement technique involves uncertainties in many areas. Uncertainties are always reduced by better measurement instrumentation, better calibration procedures, and more experimental tests. In an optical probe measurement system, major sources of uncertainty come from (1) resolutions in the sensor imaging optics and the light illumination optics, (2) resolution in the pixel image value registration in the CCD sensor, (3) noise level in the sensor signal processing electronics, (4) computation errors in the software algorithms that process the large number of image data, and (5) errors from rough calibration procedures. With reduction of uncertainties in all these areas, the accuracy of a camera imaging measurement system can be significantly improved. Maximum efficiency and accuracy may possibly be achieved by tuning the performance of critical components of the measurement system.

In this experiment, high measurement accuracy is not our primary concern. The goal of this experiment is to find out whether a camera imaging measurement system can be used to map out the complete 3D geometry of machine parts with reasonable accuracy for manufacturing purposes. After the 3D object geometry is obtained, then high accuracy measurement is certainly required in order for the camera imaging system to be used in real manufacturing applications. The camera imaging methodology uses many images taken within the restricted domain of planar features of an object to reconstruct its 3D geometry. We have shown in this experiment that our camera imaging technology can give us about 1 mm accuracy in mapping the planar features. However, 1 mm is not generally considered a reasonable manufacturing tolerance except for some crude castings. It needs approximately +/- 0.04 mm. Depending on types of application, some of the commercial state of the art video CMM probes have much better accuracy than our current system. This means that much more remain to be done to increase the accuracy of our camera probe in order for it to be practical in manufacturing use. Future work on improving the measurement accuracy of a camera imaging system can follow many possible directions, as described below.

The imaging optics inside the camera creates an image from the object. Changing the design of the imaging optics changes the image resolution and accuracy. Most influential optical parameters are the focal length and the amplification factor of the lens assembly. Properly adjusting the optical parameters is likely to increase the accuracy significantly. In certain cases, interferometry using lasers or white light may be the appropriate imaging optics to use, which will result in very high accuracy. Different lighting source patterns may also create images with different resolutions and final measurement accuracy. Using a structured lighting source has been a common way to enhance image resolution and increase accuracy. As evidence of how much difference imaging optics can make, commercial laser scanning probes have been shown to reach 0.125 μm to 1.0 μm resolution with capture ranges of 300 μm to 2000 μm.

Choosing a CCD sensor that has high resolution image pixels is necessary if high measurement accuracy is to be achieved. Commercially available state of the art CCD sensors normally have image pixels about 10 μm in size. Careful design of the electronics that processes the CCD image sensor signal to reduce the noise level may also increase the measurement accuracy noticeably. On the software side, things can be changed to improve accuracy too. Due to the large amount of image data, the computer algorithms used to analyze the image features are often simplified to compromise computation time and thus reduce computation accuracy, for faster processing. If the interest is to get the highest accuracy possible, precise computation algorithms likely exist and can be implemented to improve accuracy.

After the hardware and software of a camera imaging system are set up, the calibration procedure can also be fine tuned to yield high calibration accuracy. Most calibration errors come from uncertainties in the pre-knowledge of precise feature geometry of a calibration target, the camera model used, and the method in extracting feature geometry from the image. By precisely making the calibration target, e.g. using a coordinate measuring machine to generate a calibration target, commercial state of the art CCD camera imaging systems have been proven capable of measuring 3D object geometry within 100 μm accuracy [3]. Using a proper calibration algorithm and camera model, calibration accuracy up to 1/50 pixel is attainable although with some difficulty [7]. These very high accuracy calibration methods can be implemented into our experimental setup in the future to see how high an accuracy performance our inspection workstation can achieve.

9. Conclusions

A camera calibration procedure has been applied to a CCD camera setup used for the inspection of machine parts in the manufacturing industry. The calibration procedure yields a camera model that correlates the pixel coordinates of object features on the image plane to the physical coordinates of the corresponding features on the object. The camera model contains two sets of parameters, intrinsic and extrinsic. If both the pixel coordinates of feature point locations on the image plane and the physical corresponding feature point locations on the object can be determined with sub-pixel accuracy, then the calibration procedure will result in a camera model with sub-pixel accuracy. Presumably the key point locations in 3D space of a calibration image can be generated in many ways, for example by using a CMM or other means. In this experiment, a checkerboard image pattern was used for the calibration. The checkerboard image was generated by a computer program and printed on plain paper. The checkerboard is a planar image; however it can be placed at arbitrary 3D positions and orientations. Because of the simplicity of the checkerboard pattern, it becomes easy to obtain high accuracy corner extraction from the image and physical coordinate measurement of the corner locations. As a result of this high accuracy input data to the calibration procedure, a sub-pixel accuracy camera model has been obtained. In a region that has 0.58 mm/pixel conversion factor, a sub-pixel accuracy means that the accuracy in real dimension is better than 0.58 mm.

Once the camera model is obtained, its intrinsic parameters remain constant. However, the extrinsic parameters depend on where the objects are located in a particular application. Every time an object is relocated, its position and orientation with respect to the camera are re-determined by re-calculating the extrinsic parameters. For each particular application, a set of key feature points on the object whose coordinates are easily determined with precision is chosen to calculate the extrinsic parameters. Depending on the ability to get accurate measurement of the coordinates of feature point locations on objects and to precisely retrieve the pixel coordinates of the corresponding feature points on the object image, the re-calculated extrinsic parameters may not be as accurate as those obtained previously when the camera model was calibrated with the rather precise checkerboard image pattern. As an example of application of the calibrated camera to measure object locations and features, a machine part was used as a test specimen in the experiment. The extreme four corners on the machine part were used to re-locate the part with respect to the camera. In this experiment, a simple way of measuring the physical coordinates of the four corners only yielded a 0.5 mm accuracy. The accuracy of determining the pixel coordinates of the four part corners was about 1 to 2 pixels, due to some uncertainty in the corner features on the image. The combination of these errors resulted in a final accuracy of 1 mm to 2 mm in matching the calculated feature locations and the real feature locations on the machine part. Certainly, more elaborate ways of measuring the physical coordinates of the part corners can be used, which would possibly give higher accuracy in the measurement in the corner positions. Special feature marks may be attached to the machine part to create sharper feature images for more precise pixel coordinate extraction. While it is undesirable to attach special feature marks in some industrial production line, more sophisticated algorithms may be employed instead for precise feature extraction and feature point identification.

In principle, many types of model can be used for camera calibration. Each needs to be tested for the specific configuration of a camera setup in order to see how accurate the camera imaging system can be. In this experiment, to obtain the accuracy of our CCD camera imaging system for a machine part inspection workstation, the camera model of J.Y. Bouguet was used for calibration. As a first trial, this experiment shows good results of a satisfactorily high accuracy in a camera calibration procedure and a reasonable accuracy for the application of the calibrated camera model to locate a machine part and its features. Further tests may be conducted to show that better accuracy can be achieved in coordinate measurement of object feature locations, in extraction of feature pixel coordinates from the image, and by using other camera models.

References

1. J. Y. Bouguet, "Visual Methods for Three-Dimensional Modeling", Ph. D. Thesis, California Institute of Technology, Pasadena, California, May 1999.

2. G. P. Stein, "Internal Camera Calibration using Rotation and Geometric Shapes", M.S. Thesis, Massachusetts Institute of Technology, February 1993.

3. T. S. Shen, J. Huang, and C. H. Menq, "Multiple-sensor Integration for Rapid and High-Precision Coordinate Metrology", IEEE/ASME Transactions on Mechatronics, pp. 110 – 121, Vol.5, No.2, June 2000.

4. T. S. Shen, and C. H. Menq, "Automatic Camera Calibration for a Multiple-Sensor Integrated Coordinate Measurement System", IEEE Transactions on Robotics and Automation, pp. 502 – 507, Vol.17, No.4, August 2001.

5. M. Wilczkowiak, E. Boyer, and P. Sturm, "Camera Calibration and 3D Reconstruction from Single Images Using Parallelepipeds", Proceedings of Eighth IEEE International Conference on Computer Vision, pp.142 – 148, Vol.1, 2001.

6. R. G. Wilson and S. A. Shafer, "What is the Center of the Image?", Proceedings of IEEE Conference on Computer Vision and Pattern Recognition, pp. 670 – 671, June 1993.

7. J. Heikkila, "Geometric Camera Calibration Using Circular Control Points", IEEE Transactions on Pattern Analysis and Machine Intelligence, pp.1066 – 1077, Vol.22, No.10, October 2000.

8. P. Mansbach, "Calibration of a Camera and Light Source by Fitting to a Physical Model", Computer Vision, Graphics, and Image Processing, pp.200 – 219, Vol.35, 1986.

9. M. Boo, E. Antelo, J.D. Bruguera, "VLSI Implementation of an Edge Detector Based on Sobel Operator", Proceedings of the 20th EUROMICRO Conference on System Architecture and Integration, pp.506 – 512, Sept. 1994.

10. K.H. Hedengren, "Decomposition of Edge Operators", IEEE 9th International Conference on Pattern Recognition, pp.963 – 965, Vol.2, Nov. 1988.

11. Y. Neuvo, P. Heinonen, I. Defee, "Linear-Median Hybrid Edge Detectors", IEEE Transactions on Circuits and Systems, pp.1337 – 1343, Vol. CAS-34, No.11, Nov. 1987.

Appendices

Appendix A :   Checkerboard Calibration Images at Various Positions and Orientations
with Re-projected Corners

Figure A1 :   Checkerboard Calibration Image 1 with Re-projected Corners

Calibration Image 1

Figure A2 :   Checkerboard Calibration Image 2 with Re-projected Corners

Calibration Image 2

Figure A3 :   Checkerboard Calibration Image 3 with Re-projected Corners

Calibration Image 3

Figure A4 :   Checkerboard Calibration Image 4 with Re-projected Corners

Calibration Image 4

Figure A5 : Checkerboard Calibration Image 5 with Re-projected Corners

Calibration Image 5

Figure A6 : Checkerboard Calibration Image 6 with Re-projected Corners

Calibration Image 6

Figure A7 :   Checkerboard Calibration Image 7 with Re-projected Corners

Calibration Image 7

Figure A8 :   Checkerboard Calibration Image 8 with Re-projected Corners

Calibration Image 8

Figure A9 :   Checkerboard Calibration Image 9 with Re-projected Corners

Calibration Image 9

Figure A10 :   Checkerboard Calibration Image 10 with Re-projected Corners

Calibration Image 10

Appendix B : (1) Physical Coordinates of Corners in the Checkerboard Calibration
Image, in millimeters

(2) Pixel Coordinates of Corners in the Checkerboard Calibration Image
at Various Positions and Orientations, in pixels

(3) Extrinsic Parameters Representing Various Positions and Orientations
of the Checkerboard Calibration Image

Table B0:   Physical Coordinates of the Corners of the
             Checkerboard Calibration Image Pattern

Corner No.	Grid No.	Physical Coordinates (mm)		
1	(1, 1)	(0.00	198.53	0.00)
2	(2, 1)	(26.09	198.53	0.00)
3	(3, 1)	(52.17	198.53	0.00)
4	(4, 1)	(78.26	198.53	0.00)
5	(5, 1)	(104.34	198.53	0.00)
6	(6, 1)	(130.43	198.53	0.00)
7	(7, 1)	(156.51	198.53	0.00)
8	(8, 1)	(182.60	198.53	0.00)
9	(9, 1)	(208.69	198.53	0.00)
10	(10, 1)	(234.77	198.53	0.00)
11	(11, 1)	(260.86	198.53	0.00)
12	(1, 2)	(0.00	173.71	0.00)
13	(2, 2)	(26.09	173.71	0.00)
14	(3, 2)	(52.17	173.71	0.00)
15	(4, 2)	(78.26	173.71	0.00)
16	(5, 2)	(104.34	173.71	0.00)
17	(6, 2)	(130.43	173.71	0.00)
18	(7, 2)	(156.51	173.71	0.00)
19	(8, 2)	(182.60	173.71	0.00)
20	(9, 2)	(208.69	173.71	0.00)
21	(10, 2)	(234.77	173.71	0.00)
22	(11, 2)	(260.86	173.71	0.00)
23	(1, 3)	(0.00	148.89	0.00)
24	(2, 3)	(26.09	148.89	0.00)
25	(3, 3)	(52.17	148.89	0.00)
26	(4, 3)	(78.26	148.89	0.00)
27	(5, 3)	(104.34	148.89	0.00)
28	(6, 3)	(130.43	148.89	0.00)
29	(7, 3)	(156.51	148.89	0.00)
30	(8, 3)	(182.60	148.89	0.00)
31	(9, 3)	(208.69	148.89	0.00)
32	(10, 3)	(234.77	148.89	0.00)
33	(11, 3)	(260.86	148.89	0.00)
34	(1, 4)	(0.00	124.08	0.00)
35	(2, 4)	(26.09	124.08	0.00)
36	(3, 4)	(52.17	124.08	0.00)
37	(4, 4)	(78.26	124.08	0.00)
38	(5, 4)	(104.34	124.08	0.00)
39	(6, 4)	(130.43	124.08	0.00)
40	(7, 4)	(156.51	124.08	0.00)
41	(8, 4)	(182.60	124.08	0.00)
42	(9, 4)	(208.69	124.08	0.00)
43	(10, 4)	(234.77	124.08	0.00)
44	(11, 4)	(260.86	124.08	0.00)
45	(1, 5)	(0.00	99.26	0.00)
46	(2, 5)	(26.09	99.26	0.00)

```
47          (3,  5)          (  52.17    99.26    0.00)
48          (4,  5)          (  78.26    99.26    0.00)
49          (5,  5)          ( 104.34    99.26    0.00)
50          (6,  5)          ( 130.43    99.26    0.00)
51          (7,  5)          ( 156.51    99.26    0.00)
52          (8,  5)          ( 182.60    99.26    0.00)
53          (9,  5)          ( 208.69    99.26    0.00)
54          (10, 5)          ( 234.77    99.26    0.00)
55          (11, 5)          ( 260.86    99.26    0.00)

56          (1,  6)          (   0.00    74.45    0.00)
57          (2,  6)          (  26.09    74.45    0.00)
58          (3,  6)          (  52.17    74.45    0.00)
59          (4,  6)          (  78.26    74.45    0.00)
60          (5,  6)          ( 104.34    74.45    0.00)
61          (6,  6)          ( 130.43    74.45    0.00)
62          (7,  6)          ( 156.51    74.45    0.00)
63          (8,  6)          ( 182.60    74.45    0.00)
64          (9,  6)          ( 208.69    74.45    0.00)
65          (10, 6)          ( 234.77    74.45    0.00)
66          (11, 6)          ( 260.86    74.45    0.00)

67          (1,  7)          (   0.00    49.63    0.00)
68          (2,  7)          (  26.09    49.63    0.00)
69          (3,  7)          (  52.17    49.63    0.00)
70          (4,  7)          (  78.26    49.63    0.00)
71          (5,  7)          ( 104.34    49.63    0.00)
72          (6,  7)          ( 130.43    49.63    0.00)
73          (7,  7)          ( 156.51    49.63    0.00)
74          (8,  7)          ( 182.60    49.63    0.00)
75          (9,  7)          ( 208.69    49.63    0.00)
76          (10, 7)          ( 234.77    49.63    0.00)
77          (11, 7)          ( 260.86    49.63    0.00)

78          (1,  8)          (   0.00    24.82    0.00)
79          (2,  8)          (  26.09    24.82    0.00)
80          (3,  8)          (  52.17    24.82    0.00)
81          (4,  8)          (  78.26    24.82    0.00)
82          (5,  8)          ( 104.34    24.82    0.00)
83          (6,  8)          ( 130.43    24.82    0.00)
84          (7,  8)          ( 156.51    24.82    0.00)
85          (8,  8)          ( 182.60    24.82    0.00)
86          (9,  8)          ( 208.69    24.82    0.00)
87          (10, 8)          ( 234.77    24.82    0.00)
88          (11, 8)          ( 260.86    24.82    0.00)

89          (1,  9)          (   0.00     0.00    0.00)
90          (2,  9)          (  26.09     0.00    0.00)
91          (3,  9)          (  52.17     0.00    0.00)
92          (4,  9)          (  78.26     0.00    0.00)
93          (5,  9)          ( 104.34     0.00    0.00)
94          (6,  9)          ( 130.43     0.00    0.00)
95          (7,  9)          ( 156.51     0.00    0.00)
96          (8,  9)          ( 182.60     0.00    0.00)
97          (9,  9)          ( 208.69     0.00    0.00)
98          (10, 9)          ( 234.77     0.00    0.00)
99          (11, 9)          ( 260.86     0.00    0.00)
```

Table B1: Pixel Coordinates of the Corners of
Calibration Image 1   (pixels)

Grid (1, 1) - (11, 1)
```
   (103.6  359.0)      (144.8  360.2)      (185.5  361.0)      (226.6  361.5)
   (268.0  362.1)      (309.5  362.5)      (350.8  362.8)      (392.3  362.9)
   (433.2  362.6)      (473.9  362.3)      (513.8  361.9)
```

Grid (1, 2) - (11, 2)
```
   (102.7  320.8)      (144.4  321.5)      (185.3  322.0)      (226.6  322.6)
   (268.3  323.1)      (309.6  323.5)      (351.1  323.6)      (393.1  323.9)
   (434.3  324.1)      (474.7  323.8)      (514.7  323.5)
```

Grid (1, 3) - (11, 3)
```
   (102.8  281.5)      (144.6  282.2)      (185.2  282.7)      (226.4  283.3)
   (268.3  283.5)      (309.7  283.9)      (351.7  284.3)      (393.1  284.5)
   (434.3  284.6)      (475.4  284.7)      (515.5  284.7)
```

Grid (1, 4) - (11, 4)
```
   (102.6  242.7)      (144.4  243.0)      (185.2  243.4)      (226.7  243.6)
   (268.4  244.2)      (310.0  244.5)      (351.9  244.6)      (393.3  245.2)
   (434.9  245.4)      (475.6  245.5)      (516.3  245.8)
```

Grid (1, 5) - (11, 5)
```
   (103.1  203.4)      (144.8  203.7)      (185.9  204.0)      (227.3  204.4)
   (268.5  204.5)      (310.6  204.9)      (352.1  205.5)      (394.2  205.6)
   (435.3  206.1)      (476.1  206.5)      (516.4  206.8)
```

Grid (1, 6) - (11, 6)
```
   (103.6  164.8)      (145.1  164.6)      (186.1  164.6)      (227.3  164.8)
   (268.8  165.2)      (310.8  165.5)      (352.4  165.7)      (394.2  166.4)
   (435.3  166.7)      (476.4  167.5)      (516.5  168.0)
```

Grid (1, 7) - (11, 7)
```
   (104.5  125.3)      (145.8  125.2)      (186.7  125.3)      (228.1  125.5)
   (269.5  125.5)      (310.9  126.1)      (352.9  126.5)      (394.2  127.0)
   (435.5  127.5)      (476.4  128.2)      (516.6  129.1)
```

Grid (1, 8) - (11, 8)
```
   (105.3   86.9)      (146.6   86.2)      (187.4   86.2)      (228.5   86.3)
   (269.9   86.4)      (311.6   86.6)      (353.0   87.3)      (394.5   87.7)
   (435.7   88.4)      (476.5   89.3)      (516.7   90.3)
```

Grid (1, 9) - (11, 9)
```
   (106.5   47.9)      (147.6   47.3)      (188.2   47.3)      (229.4   47.3)
   (270.5   47.5)      (312.0   47.4)      (353.3   47.9)      (395.0   48.6)
   (435.7   49.5)      (476.3   50.8)      (516.1   51.9)
```

Table B2:   Pixel Coordinates of the Corners of
Calibration Image 2   (pixels)

Grid (1, 1) - (11, 1)
```
  ( 97.6   373.5)      (140.0   374.2)      (181.5   374.4)      (223.7   374.2)
  (266.2   374.1)      (308.4   373.9)      (350.8   373.7)      (393.5   373.2)
  (435.4   371.7)      (477.2   370.5)      (518.1   369.2)
```

Grid (1, 2) - (11, 2)
```
  ( 93.7   337.3)      (136.5   337.2)      (178.9   336.9)      (221.7   336.6)
  (264.8   336.5)      (307.6   336.3)      (350.8   336.1)      (394.2   335.6)
  (437.0   335.0)      (479.1   333.8)      (520.7   332.3)
```

Grid (1, 3) - (11, 3)
```
  ( 90.0   298.2)      (133.4   298.2)      (176.0   298.4)      (219.4   298.3)
  (262.9   298.0)      (307.3   297.5)      (350.7   296.8)      (394.5   296.5)
  (438.0   295.9)      (481.1   295.4)      (523.4   294.4)
```

Grid (1, 4) - (11, 4)
```
  ( 86.0   259.2)      (130.1   258.9)      (173.4   258.6)      (217.2   258.5)
  (261.7   258.0)      (306.2   257.5)      (350.7   256.9)      (395.3   256.5)
  (438.8   256.1)      (482.6   255.5)      (525.7   254.8)
```

Grid (1, 5) - (11, 5)
```
  ( 82.2   218.6)      (126.9   218.2)      (171.2   217.7)      (215.8   217.4)
  (260.4   216.9)      (305.4   216.5)      (350.7   216.1)      (395.4   215.5)
  (440.0   215.3)      (484.3   214.6)      (527.6   214.3)
```

Grid (1, 6) - (11, 6)
```
  ( 79.3   177.4)      (124.2   176.6)      (168.7   175.9)      (213.7   175.5)
  (259.3   174.9)      (305.1   174.5)      (350.8   174.1)      (396.4   173.5)
  (441.1   173.4)      (485.8   173.2)      (529.8   173.0)
```

Grid (1, 7) - (11, 7)
```
  ( 76.0   134.6)      (121.3   133.8)      (166.4   133.0)      (212.2   132.3)
  (258.2   131.7)      (304.1   131.2)      (350.6   130.8)      (396.4   130.5)
  (442.2   130.6)      (487.5   130.5)      (531.7   130.6)
```

Grid (1, 8) - (11, 8)
```
  ( 72.9    91.4)      (118.7    90.1)      (164.3    89.0)      (210.5    88.2)
  (257.0    87.4)      (303.9    87.0)      (350.5    86.6)      (397.0    86.5)
  (443.2    86.6)      (488.8    86.8)      (533.7    87.2)
```

Grid (1, 9) - (11, 9)
```
  ( 70.4    47.2)      (116.5    45.7)      (162.4    44.5)      (209.1    43.5)
  (256.1    42.8)      (302.9    42.3)      (350.4    42.1)      (397.5    41.9)
  (444.1    42.1)      (489.8    42.6)      (535.1    43.2)
```

Table B3: Pixel Coordinates of the Corners of
Calibration Image 3   (pixels)

Grid (1, 1) - (11, 1)
  (57.9   391.1)   (103.7   393.0)   (149.3   394.3)   (195.7   395.5)
  (242.5   396.5)   (289.6   397.2)   (336.9   397.5)   (384.0   397.8)
  (430.6   397.8)   (476.6   397.7)   (522.1   397.3)

Grid (1, 2) - (11, 2)
  (60.1   347.5)   (106.2   348.8)   (151.7   350.0)   (197.6   351.9)
  (243.9   351.8)   (290.3   352.5)   (337.1   352.8)   (383.9   353.3)
  (430.2   353.4)   (475.8   353.5)   (520.6   353.4)

Grid (1, 3) - (11, 3)
  (64.3   304.2)   (109.3   305.4)   (154.1   306.3)   (199.3   307.1)
  (245.1   307.7)   (291.3   308.5)   (337.2   309.1)   (383.7   309.5)
  (429.5   309.5)   (474.7   309.6)   (519.3   309.8)

Grid (1, 4) - (11, 4)
  (67.2   262.2)   (112.2   262.9)   (156.4   263.5)   (201.2   264.3)
  (246.8   264.7)   (292.4   265.5)   (338.0   266.2)   (383.4   266.5)
  (428.5   266.8)   (473.1   267.4)   (517.4   267.6)

Grid (1, 5) - (11, 5)
  (70.9   221.0)   (115.2   221.4)   (159.1   222.1)   (203.3   222.5)
  (248.1   223.1)   (293.3   223.5)   (338.2   224.4)   (382.8   224.7)
  (427.4   225.5)   (471.9   225.8)   (515.4   226.5)

Grid (1, 6) - (11, 6)
  (74.8   181.2)   (118.5   181.1)   (162.0   181.5)   (205.5   181.9)
  (249.9   182.3)   (294.0   182.7)   (338.2   183.4)   (382.7   184.3)
  (426.8   184.7)   (470.4   185.5)   (513.2   186.3)

Grid (1, 7) - (11, 7)
  (79.1   141.7)   (122.0   141.8)   (164.8   142.1)   (207.8   142.4)
  (251.3   142.5)   (294.8   143.4)   (339.0   143.5)   (382.7   144.5)
  (426.2   145.0)   (468.8   145.8)   (511.1   147.0)

Grid (1, 8) - (11, 8)
  (83.0   104.0)   (125.6   103.4)   (167.7   103.5)   (210.3   103.9)
  (253.2   104.3)   (296.1   104.6)   (339.3   105.3)   (382.4   105.8)
  (425.1   106.5)   (467.3   107.6)   (509.1   108.8)

Grid (1, 9) - (11, 9)
  (87.7   66.6)   (129.6   65.8)   (170.7   65.8)   (212.9   66.3)
  (254.7   66.5)   (297.3   66.3)   (339.4   67.1)   (382.2   67.8)
  (423.8   68.9)   (465.5   70.5)   (506.3   71.5)

Table B4: Pixel Coordinates of the Corners of
Calibration Image 4 (pixels)

Grid (1, 1) - (11, 1)
    (95.9   416.8)   (144.4   415.2)   (191.4   413.1)   (237.4   410.6)
    (282.4   408.2)   (326.6   405.5)   (369.3   403.1)   (410.8   400.1)
    (450.3   396.8)   (488.8   395.1)   (524.7   391.3)

Grid (1, 2) - (11, 2)
    (94.8   373.2)   (143.3   371.4)   (190.6   369.6)   (236.7   367.7)
    (282.2   365.8)   (326.2   363.7)   (369.2   361.7)   (411.2   359.6)
    (451.2   357.3)   (489.3   355.0)   (526.2   352.3)

Grid (1, 3) - (11, 3)
    (93.9   327.9)   (142.6   326.8)   (189.7   325.6)   (236.4   324.5)
    (282.1   323.1)   (326.0   321.5)   (369.1   320.0)   (411.1   318.5)
    (451.3   316.8)   (490.2   315.3)   (526.9   313.4)

Grid (1, 4) - (11, 4)
    (93.3   282.9)   (142.0   282.3)   (189.5   281.5)   (236.3   280.6)
    (281.7   280.0)   (325.7   279.1)   (369.0   278.3)   (410.8   277.3)
    (451.2   276.4)   (490.1   275.3)   (527.2   274.3)

Grid (1, 5) - (11, 5)
    (92.6   237.5)   (141.6   237.4)   (189.3   237.2)   (235.8   237.0)
    (281.3   236.6)   (325.7   236.5)   (369.1   236.4)   (410.8   236.0)
    (451.2   235.6)   (489.9   235.4)   (527.0   235.2)

Grid (1, 6) - (11, 6)
    (92.5   192.6)   (141.6   192.5)   (189.2   192.8)   (235.8   193.3)
    (281.4   193.5)   (325.6   193.7)   (369.1   194.4)   (410.8   194.5)
    (451.3   195.2)   (490.1   195.5)   (527.1   196.1)

Grid (1, 7) - (11, 7)
    (93.3   147.0)   (141.9   147.7)   (189.4   148.5)   (235.9   149.4)
    (281.5   150.3)   (325.6   151.4)   (369.1   152.4)   (410.8   153.4)
    (451.3   154.5)   (490.2   155.4)   (527.3   156.7)

Grid (1, 8) - (11, 8)
    (93.5   102.0)   (142.4   102.9)   (189.6   104.2)   (236.2   105.6)
    (281.4   107.1)   (325.7   108.5)   (369.0   110.4)   (410.8   112.1)
    (451.2   113.7)   (489.9   115.5)   (527.1   117.4)

Grid (1, 9) - (11, 9)
    (94.2   57.4)   (143.1   58.9)   (190.2   60.5)   (236.5   62.4)
    (281.7   64.4)   (326.1   66.3)   (369.1   68.4)   (410.9   71.1)
    (450.8   73.3)   (489.2   76.2)   (526.2   78.2)

Table B5: Pixel Coordinates of the Corners of Calibration Image 5 (pixels)

Grid (1, 1) - (11, 1)
```
(114.6  392.9)      (153.0  398.0)      (191.4  399.4)      (231.5  402.0)
(272.7  404.7)      (315.2  407.5)      (358.7  410.3)      (403.5  412.4)
(449.4  414.3)      (496.0  416.1)      (543.1  417.6)
```

Grid (1, 2) - (11, 2)
```
(113.1  354.9)      (152.0  356.9)      (190.9  359.2)      (231.2  361.5)
(272.6  363.6)      (315.2  365.6)      (358.7  367.7)      (403.9  369.7)
(449.9  371.5)      (496.6  372.8)      (544.1  373.9)
```

Grid (1, 3) - (11, 3)
```
(113.3  315.3)      (151.9  317.2)      (190.7  318.7)      (230.6  320.5)
(271.9  322.2)      (315.3  323.5)      (358.8  324.7)      (404.4  326.4)
(450.3  327.5)      (497.2  328.6)      (544.8  329.5)
```

Grid (1, 4) - (11, 4)
```
(113.1  276.3)      (151.5  277.2)      (190.0  278.2)      (230.4  279.2)
(271.9  280.1)      (315.2  281.0)      (358.9  281.7)      (404.4  282.5)
(450.5  283.4)      (497.6  284.0)      (545.3  284.5)
```

Grid (1, 5) - (11, 5)
```
(112.7  236.6)      (151.3  237.2)      (190.0  237.5)      (230.5  237.7)
(271.8  238.1)      (314.8  238.4)      (358.9  238.6)      (404.4  238.8)
(450.9  239.2)      (498.0  239.4)      (545.5  239.5)
```

Grid (1, 6) - (11, 6)
```
(113.1  197.6)      (151.4  197.2)      (190.2  196.6)      (230.3  196.4)
(271.8  196.0)      (315.0  195.5)      (358.8  195.5)      (404.5  195.2)
(450.9  194.8)      (498.1  194.6)      (545.6  194.5)
```

Grid (1, 7) - (11, 7)
```
(113.3  157.9)      (151.4  156.8)      (190.3  155.8)      (230.5  154.8)
(271.9  153.7)      (315.3  152.8)      (358.8  152.0)      (404.5  151.3)
(450.5  150.4)      (497.8  149.7)      (545.4  149.3)
```

Grid (1, 8) - (11, 8)
```
(113.5  118.8)      (151.6  116.8)      (190.4  115.0)      (230.7  113.4)
(272.2  111.6)      (315.3  110.3)      (359.0  109.6)      (404.4  107.5)
(450.4  106.2)      (497.4  105.1)      (545.1  104.1)
```

Grid (1, 9) - (11, 9)
```
(114.4   79.4)      (152.4   76.4)      (190.8   74.5)      (231.2   72.2)
(272.3   70.2)      (314.8   67.7)      (358.7   65.7)      (404.1   63.9)
(450.2   62.3)      (497.0   61.1)      (544.4   59.8)
```

Table B6: Pixel Coordinates of the Corners of
Calibration Image 6   (pixels)

Grid (1, 1) - (11, 1)
  (78.9   408.8)   (124.6   410.8)   (169.8   412.1)   (215.9   412.8)
  (262.1   413.4)   (308.5   414.0)   (355.1   414.5)   (401.2   414.5)
  (447.0   413.8)   (492.2   413.2)   (536.6   412.3)

Grid (1, 2) - (11, 2)
  (77.7   366.9)   (123.8   368.0)   (169.6   368.7)   (215.8   369.5)
  (262.1   370.2)   (308.5   370.6)   (355.3   371.0)   (402.2   371.3)
  (448.1   371.1)   (493.4   370.6)   (537.9   369.9)

Grid (1, 3) - (11, 3)
  (77.7   323.1)   (123.7   324.1)   (169.3   324.9)   (215.6   325.6)
  (262.0   326.4)   (308.8   326.5)   (355.4   326.9)   (402.2   327.2)
  (448.7   327.3)   (494.5   327.3)   (539.4   326.8)

Grid (1, 4) - (11, 4)
  (77.2   279.7)   (123.4   280.2)   (169.1   280.8)   (215.7   281.5)
  (262.4   282.0)   (309.4   282.4)   (356.3   282.6)   (403.1   282.9)
  (449.1   283.3)   (494.9   283.4)   (539.8   283.3)

Grid (1, 5) - (11, 5)
  (77.3   235.6)   (123.5   236.3)   (169.4   236.6)   (215.9   237.3)
  (262.7   237.5)   (309.6   238.1)   (356.4   238.5)   (403.3   238.6)
  (449.5   239.2)   (495.3   239.5)   (540.4   239.6)

Grid (1, 6) - (11, 6)
  (77.7   192.4)   (124.1   192.3)   (169.9   192.5)   (216.1   192.7)
  (262.7   193.3)   (309.7   193.5)   (356.6   193.9)   (403.6   194.5)
  (450.2   195.0)   (495.9   195.5)   (540.8   196.2)

Grid (1, 7) - (11, 7)
  (78.6   148.0)   (124.5   148.1)   (170.4   148.2)   (216.8   148.4)
  (263.4   148.6)   (310.5   149.2)   (357.5   149.5)   (404.3   150.2)
  (450.4   150.7)   (496.2   151.5)   (541.1   152.4)

Grid (1, 8) - (11, 8)
  (79.4   104.5)   (125.5   104.1)   (171.2   104.0)   (217.5   104.2)
  (264.0   104.3)   (310.7   104.7)   (357.6   105.3)   (404.4   105.9)
  (450.4   106.5)   (496.2   107.6)   (541.2   108.7)

Grid (1, 9) - (11, 9)
  (80.9   61.2)   (126.6   60.7)   (172.2   60.4)   (218.4   60.4)
  (264.7   60.5)   (311.2   60.5)   (357.8   61.2)   (404.5   62.1)
  (450.5   63.1)   (495.8   64.5)   (540.6   65.9)

Table B7: Pixel Coordinates of the Corners of
Calibration Image 7 (pixels)

Grid (1, 1) – (11, 1)
  (80.7 438.0)   (127.2 439.8)   (172.9 440.8)   (219.6 441.1)
  (266.3 441.4)   (313.3 441.5)   (360.4 441.9)   (407.4 441.2)
  (453.5 439.7)   (499.3 438.4)   (544.3 436.7)

Grid (1, 2) – (11, 2)
  (76.1 400.3)   (122.5 401.2)   (169.7 401.5)   (217.2 401.9)
  (265.0 402.3)   (313.1 402.4)   (361.0 402.5)   (409.1 402.3)
  (456.3 401.6)   (503.1 400.2)   (548.7 398.4)

Grid (1, 3) – (11, 3)
  (70.2 359.1)   (118.5 359.8)   (166.1 360.6)   (214.5 361.4)
  (263.4 361.6)   (312.5 361.4)   (361.3 361.2)   (410.3 360.8)
  (458.8 360.5)   (506.7 359.9)   (553.5 358.6)

Grid (1, 4) – (11, 4)
  (66.1 317.2)   (114.1 317.6)   (162.6 318.2)   (212.3 318.5)
  (261.8 318.6)   (312.0 318.5)   (362.2 318.5)   (412.2 318.1)
  (461.5 317.7)   (510.1 317.4)   (557.7 316.5)

Grid (1, 5) – (11, 5)
  (59.9 273.1)   (109.7 273.4)   (159.5 273.6)   (209.9 273.6)
  (260.5 274.3)   (311.7 274.4)   (362.5 274.0)   (413.6 273.6)
  (463.8 273.5)   (513.3 273.2)   (562.1 272.5)

Grid (1, 6) – (11, 6)
  (56.2 227.6)   (105.9 227.6)   (156.3 227.5)   (207.6 227.6)
  (259.3 227.9)   (311.2 227.7)   (363.3 227.7)   (415.2 227.5)
  (466.3 227.5)   (516.8 227.5)   (566.3 227.5)

Grid (1, 7) – (11, 7)
  (50.7 180.0)   (101.9 180.1)   (153.2 179.6)   (205.3 179.5)
  (258.1 179.6)   (310.8 179.4)   (363.9 179.5)   (416.9 179.6)
  (468.9 180.2)   (520.3 180.5)   (570.6 180.5)

Grid (1, 8) – (11, 8)
  (47.4 131.3)   (98.2 130.7)   (150.3 130.1)   (203.3 129.7)
  (256.9 129.5)   (310.6 129.5)   (364.4 129.6)   (418.2 130.1)
  (471.3 130.4)   (523.6 131.1)   (574.7 131.8)

Grid (1, 9) – (11, 9)
  (43.1 81.2)   (94.8 80.1)   (147.7 79.2)   (201.6 78.6)
  (255.7 78.4)   (310.4 78.4)   (365.3 78.6)   (419.6 79.1)
  (473.5 79.7)   (526.3 80.6)   (578.2 81.6)

Table B8: Pixel Coordinates of the Corners of
Calibration Image 8 (pixels)

Grid (1, 1) - (11, 1)
      (49.9   397.5)   (100.3   400.9)   (151.9   403.8)   (204.5   406.6)
      (257.5   409.1)   (310.8   411.3)   (364.6   413.1)   (418.3   414.6)
      (471.0   415.9)   (523.0   416.8)   (573.9   417.4)

Grid (1, 2) - (11, 2)
      (53.7   348.2)   (104.7   351.0)   (156.0   353.7)   (208.1   356.4)
      (260.4   358.5)   (313.1   360.7)   (365.8   362.4)   (419.2   364.1)
      (471.3   365.4)   (522.5   366.6)   (572.7   367.6)

Grid (1, 3) - (11, 3)
      (60.4   299.7)   (109.8   302.2)   (160.1   304.5)   (211.3   306.6)
      (262.8   308.8)   (315.3   311.0)   (367.3   312.7)   (419.4   314.5)
      (470.9   315.9)   (522.1   317.4)   (571.6   318.6)

Grid (1, 4) - (11, 4)
      (64.8   252.6)   (114.6   254.5)   (164.3   256.5)   (214.8   258.5)
      (266.2   260.5)   (317.4   262.5)   (368.7   264.5)   (419.9   266.5)
      (470.6   268.2)   (520.6   269.5)   (569.6   271.4)

Grid (1, 5) - (11, 5)
      (70.8   206.7)   (119.7   208.5)   (168.8   210.4)   (218.5   212.4)
      (268.6   213.9)   (319.2   215.6)   (370.0   217.8)   (420.3   219.7)
      (469.8   221.5)   (519.1   223.5)   (567.3   225.5)

Grid (1, 6) - (11, 6)
      (76.5   162.9)   (125.2   164.1)   (173.4   165.6)   (222.3   167.3)
      (271.8   168.7)   (321.1   170.5)   (371.2   172.5)   (420.4   174.6)
      (469.5   176.6)   (517.7   178.7)   (565.2   181.1)

Grid (1, 7) - (11, 7)
      (82.9   119.6)   (130.4   120.8)   (177.9   122.3)   (226.1   123.7)
      (274.4   125.2)   (323.3   127.3)   (372.2   128.9)   (420.5   131.3)
      (468.7   133.1)   (516.4   135.3)   (562.8   138.0)

Grid (1, 8) - (11, 8)
      (88.8   78.4)   (135.8   79.2)   (182.5   80.3)   (229.8   82.0)
      (277.5   83.5)   (325.3   85.2)   (372.9   87.1)   (420.6   89.2)
      (467.9   91.3)   (514.5   93.7)   (560.4   96.4)

Grid (1, 9) - (11, 9)
      (95.4   38.7)   (141.5   39.2)   (187.2   40.3)   (233.6   41.7)
      (280.2   43.0)   (326.8   44.1)   (373.8   46.0)   (420.8   48.4)
      (467.0   50.7)   (512.7   54.2)   (557.5   56.4)

Table B9: Pixel Coordinates of the Corners of Calibration Image 9 (pixels)

```
Grid (1, 1) - (11, 1)
  ( 54.1  451.5)    (107.4  450.3)    (160.4  448.6)    (212.6  446.2)
  (263.7  443.7)    (313.9  441.0)    (362.3  438.4)    (409.4  435.1)
  (453.6  431.5)    (496.8  427.8)    (538.1  423.9)

Grid (1, 2) - (11, 2)
  ( 52.5  402.7)    (106.3  401.6)    (159.7  400.0)    (212.4  398.4)
  (263.9  396.4)    (314.2  394.4)    (362.8  392.3)    (410.2  389.9)
  (455.5  387.4)    (498.4  384.6)    (540.1  381.1)

Grid (1, 3) - (11, 3)
  ( 51.3  352.2)    (105.5  351.5)    (159.2  350.7)    (212.3  349.7)
  (263.9  348.5)    (314.2  346.9)    (363.3  345.4)    (410.4  343.6)
  (456.1  341.9)    (499.7  340.1)    (541.5  337.9)

Grid (1, 4) - (11, 4)
  ( 50.6  301.4)    (105.0  301.3)    (159.0  300.8)    (212.3  300.4)
  (264.1  299.7)    (314.4  299.0)    (363.4  298.3)    (411.2  297.4)
  (456.8  296.4)    (500.5  295.4)    (542.2  294.4)

Grid (1, 5) - (11, 5)
  ( 50.2  250.3)    (110.1  249.7)    (159.2  250.5)    (212.4  250.6)
  (264.5  250.7)    (315.3  250.8)    (364.3  250.7)    (411.5  250.6)
  (457.1  250.6)    (500.8  250.5)    (542.6  250.3)

Grid (1, 6) - (11, 6)
  ( 50.9  198.9)    (105.3  199.5)    (159.6  200.4)    (212.9  201.0)
  (265.1  201.6)    (315.6  202.5)    (364.7  203.4)    (412.4  204.1)
  (458.1  204.6)    (501.6  205.5)    (543.2  206.4)

Grid (1, 7) - (11, 7)
  ( 51.4  147.4)    (106.0  148.4)    (160.3  149.7)    (213.5  151.2)
  (265.6  152.5)    (316.3  154.1)    (365.5  155.5)    (412.6  157.3)
  (458.5  158.7)    (502.2  160.4)    (543.9  162.1)

Grid (1, 8) - (11, 8)
  ( 52.9   96.0)    (107.2   97.4)    (161.3   99.2)    (214.4  101.3)
  (266.2  103.4)    (316.6  105.6)    (365.6  108.0)    (413.3  110.4)
  (458.6  112.9)    (502.3  115.4)    (544.2  118.0)

Grid (1, 9) - (11, 9)
  ( 54.8   45.5)    (108.6   47.2)    (162.6   49.5)    (215.5   52.2)
  (267.2   54.9)    (317.6   57.5)    (366.6   60.7)    (413.7   64.1)
  (459.1   67.4)    (502.2   71.1)    (543.5   74.5)
```

Table B10: Pixel Coordinates of the Corners of
Calibration Image 10 (pixels)

Grid (1, 1) - (11, 1)
  (73.4   410.7)   (115.4 416.8)   (157.6 419.1)   (202.1 422.4)
  (247.8 426.2)   (295.5 429.6)   (344.0 433.3)   (394.8 436.2)
  (446.3 438.6)   (498.6 440.9)   (551.6 442.9)

Grid (1, 2) - (11, 2)
  (71.5   368.4)   (114.4 371.3)   (157.3 374.2)   (201.8 377.3)
  (247.8 380.2)   (295.7 383.0)   (344.9 385.8)   (395.3 388.3)
  (447.1 390.6)   (499.9 392.4)   (553.2 393.9)

Grid (1, 3) - (11, 3)
  (71.7   324.4)   (114.2 326.9)   (156.7 329.2)   (201.2 331.5)
  (247.6 333.5)   (295.8 335.5)   (345.0 337.5)   (396.2 339.5)
  (447.9 341.2)   (500.8 342.6)   (554.5 344.0)

Grid (1, 4) - (11, 4)
  (71.6   281.1)   (113.9 282.2)   (156.4 283.6)   (201.1 285.2)
  (247.8 286.5)   (295.8 287.7)   (345.2 289.1)   (396.4 290.4)
  (448.6 291.4)   (501.6 292.5)   (555.5 293.4)

Grid (1, 5) - (11, 5)
  (71.7   236.7)   (114.0 237.5)   (156.7 238.2)   (201.6 238.6)
  (247.9 239.4)   (295.8 239.7)   (345.8 240.5)   (396.9 241.0)
  (449.1 241.5)   (502.1 242.1)   (556.0 242.5)

Grid (1, 6) - (11, 6)
  (72.4   193.3)   (114.3 192.8)   (157.3 192.5)   (201.8 192.3)
  (247.9 192.0)   (296.2 191.7)   (346.1 191.6)   (397.4 191.6)
  (449.2 191.5)   (502.5 191.5)   (556.3 191.6)

Grid (1, 7) - (11, 7)
  (73.1   149.1)   (114.9 148.0)   (157.7 146.8)   (202.4 145.7)
  (248.6 144.6)   (297.0 143.8)   (346.2 143.0)   (397.6 142.3)
  (449.3 141.5)   (502.5 141.0)   (556.4 140.6)

Grid (1, 8) - (11, 8)
  (73.9   105.7)   (115.8 103.2)   (158.5 101.3)   (203.2   99.5)
  (249.3   97.6)   (297.2   96.0)   (346.4   94.4)   (397.5   93.0)
  (449.3   91.7)   (502.3   90.7)   (555.9   90.0)

Grid (1, 9) - (11, 9)
  (75.6   62.0)   (117.0   59.2)   (159.5   56.5)   (204.1   53.9)
  (250.0   51.3)   (297.2   48.5)   (346.3   46.3)   (397.5   44.3)
  (449.1   42.7)   (501.9   41.4)   (555.3   40.4)

Table B11:   Extrinsic Parameters for the 10 Calibration Images

Image No. 1

       Tc =   (-147.9   -112.4   477.8)   mm
       Omc =   (0.00437   -0.0196   0.00813)   radians

                ⎛   0.999   -0.00817   -0.0196   ⎞
       Rc =   ⎜   0.00809   0.999   -0.00445 ⎟
                ⎝   0.0196   0.00429   0.999   ⎠

Image No. 2

       Tc =   (-150.6   -99.7   419.3)   mm
       Omc =   (0.240   -0.0194   -0.00739)   radians

                ⎛   0.999   0.00499   -0.0201   ⎞
       Rc =   ⎜ -0.00964   0.971   -0.238   ⎟
                ⎝   0.0184   0.238   0.971   ⎠

Image No. 3

       Tc =   (-156.6   -98.4   467.5)   mm
       Omc =   (-0.242   -0.0191   0.0101)   radians

                ⎛   0.999   -0.00768   -0.0201   ⎞
       Rc =   ⎜   0.0123   0.971   0.239   ⎟
                ⎝   0.0177   -0.239   0.971   ⎠

Image No. 4

       Tc =   (-134.2   -91.9   412.0)   mm
       Omc =   (0.00443   -0.257   -0.00115)   radians

                ⎛   0.967   0.000569   -0.254   ⎞
       Rc =   ⎜ -0.00170   0.999   -0.00423 ⎟
                ⎝   0.254   0.00453   0.967   ⎠

Image No. 5

       Tc =   (-141.3   -91.4   474.2)   mm
       Omc =   (0.00389   0.228   0.00129)   radians

                ⎛   0.974   -0.000836   0.226   ⎞
       Rc =   ⎜   0.00172   0.999   -0.00371 ⎟
                ⎝ -0.226   0.00400   0.974   ⎠

Image No. 6

    Tc =   (-146.3   -92.8   424.9)   mm
    Omc =   (0.00263 -0.0183 0.00869)   radians

             ⎡ 0.999   -0.00872   -0.0182 ⎤
    Rc =   ⎢ 0.00867   0.999   -0.00271 ⎥
             ⎣ 0.0183   0.00255   0.999   ⎦

Image No. 7

    Tc =   (-144.3   -69.8   363.3)   mm
    Omc =   (0.284   -0.0151   0.00193)   radians

             ⎡ 0.999   -0.00403   -0.01461 ⎤
    Rc =   ⎢ -0.000219   0.960   -0.280   ⎥
             ⎣ 0.0152   0.280   0.960   ⎦

Image No. 8

    Tc =   (-137.4   -104.8   422.8)   mm
    Omc =   (-0.269   -0.0120   0.0364)   radians

             ⎡ 0.999   -0.0343   -0.0168 ⎤
    Rc =   ⎢ 0.0376   0.963   0.266   ⎥
             ⎣ 0.00703   -0.266   0.964   ⎦

Image No. 9

    Tc =   (-137.9   -86.8   360.7)   mm
    Omc =   (0.00880   -0.248   0.00943)   radians

             ⎡ 0.969   -0.0104   -0.245   ⎤
    Rc =   ⎢ 0.00825   0.999   -0.00987 ⎥
             ⎣ 0.246   0.00754   0.969   ⎦

Image No. 10

    Tc =   (-149.2   -92.1   423.8)   mm
    Omc =   (-0.00251   0.215   0.00660)   radians

             ⎡ 0.977   -0.00682   0.213   ⎤
    Rc =   ⎢ 0.00628   0.999   0.00319 ⎥
             ⎣ -0.213   -0.00178   0.977   ⎦

Appendix C :   (1) Machine Part Images at Two Locations

                       (2) Extracted Edges of the Machine Part Images at Two Locations

                       (3) Mapped Features of the Machine Part at Two Locations

Figure C1 :   Machine Part Image at Negative Tilt 24.0°

Figure C2 :   Machine Part Image at Positive Tilt 25.4°

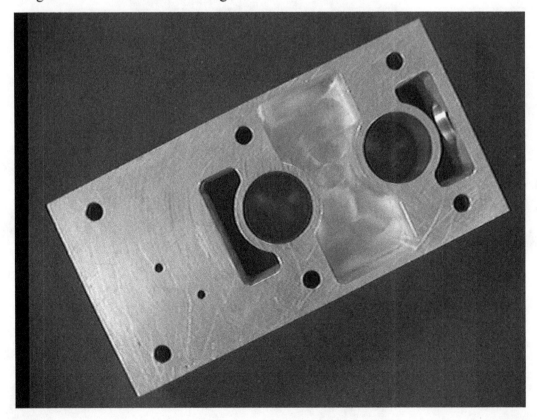

Figure C3 :   Edges Detected of the Machine Part at Negative Tilt 24.0°

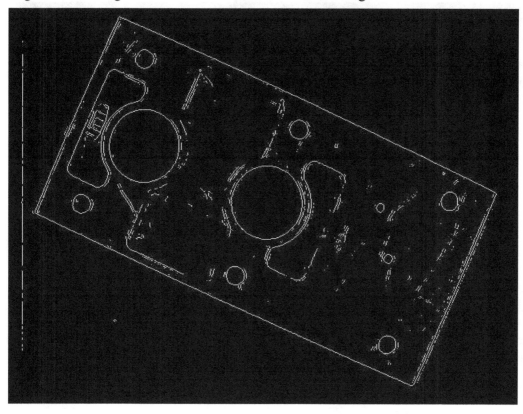

Figure C4 : Edges Detected of the Machine Part at Positive Tilt 25.4°

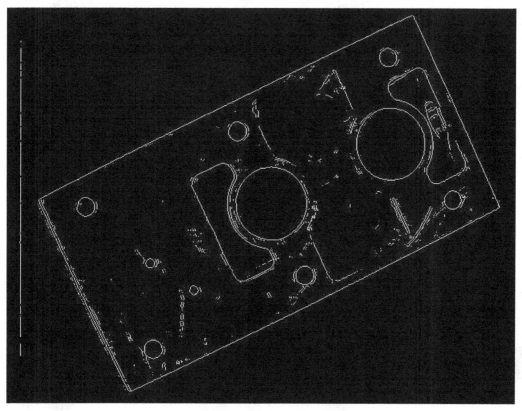

Figure C5 : Matched Features of the Machine Part at Negative Tilt 24.0°

Figure C6 : Matched Features of the Machine Part at Positive Tilt 25.4°

www.ingramcontent.com/pod-product-compliance
Lightning Source LLC
Chambersburg PA
CBHW080603060326
40689CB00021B/4925